The Open Systems Development Life Cycle

Lean Agile Project and Program Management

SOP 1000-01

For Sandy

With special thanks to the love of my life my wife Alison.

To my children: Give.

PROCEDURE OVERVIEW

PROGRAM/PROJECT MANAGEMENT PROCEDURE defines the project management infrastructure, reporting relationships and project management activities within SDLC.com. *Project Managers*, *Program Managers* and the *Program Management Office (PMO)* are the components that deliver project management.

PROGRAM/PROJECT MANAGEMENT refers to the systematic execution of a System Development Life Cycle (SDLC) for a release or projects that have significant impact on an organization's service delivery. This procedure oversees the SDLC execution; thus, it relies heavily on defined procedure activities and acceptance criteria for inputs and outputs.

THE *PROJECT MANAGER* is the focal point throughout a project who ensures that the responsible party has completed with quality and comply with defined acceptance criteria. The *Project Manager* also acts as the conduit for communicating the progress of the project and decisions made throughout the process to the *Project Sponsor*, *Contracting Organization*, and the *Performing Organization*.

PROGRAM MANAGEMENT addresses oversight for a group of projects. *Program Managers* shoulder the responsible for the successful completion of program objectives by supporting and developing project staff. Reporting at this level provides *Executive Management* with the information necessary to make informed decisions and execute actions that optimize benefits to the organization.

The *Program Manager* is the tactical manager who facilitates, monitors and communicates the progress and issues in implementing the strategic objectives of an approved program. The *Program Manager* works cross-functionally to develop the blueprint that integrates multiple release deliverables that enhance the program's portfolio.

The *PMO* s the organization that consolidates all project plans and reports the status to executive management. Impacts from individual projects can be seen from an organizational perspective and responded to rapidly. The *PMO* is where project and program standards, procedures, policies and reporting are established.

Every unit within SDLC.com interacts with **PROGRAM/PROJECT MANAGEMENT**. Every release of new and enhanced features and functionality requires the commitment and effort from all departments.

Procedure Owner: Chief Technology Officer

Table of Contents

REVISION HISTORY

Version	Date	Author	Description

Distribution List:

PROCEDURE DIAGRAM
(See Appendix 1 for a detailed process view)

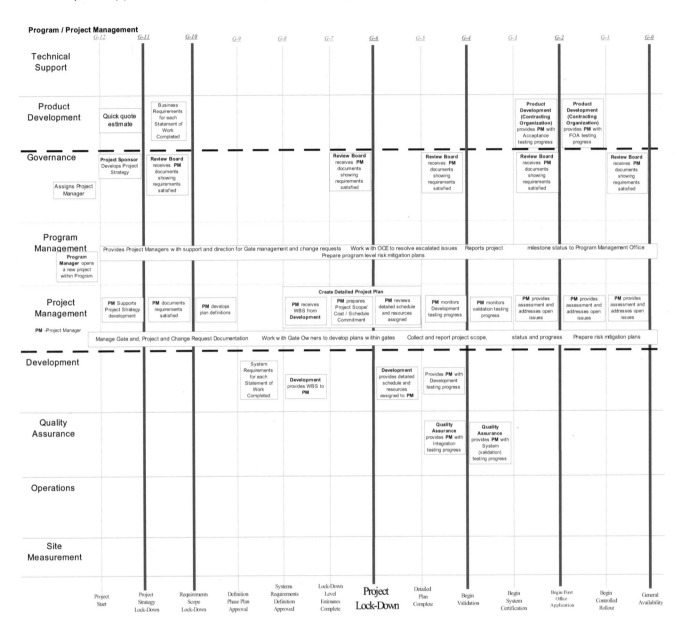

ROLES AND RESPONSIBILITIES

Contracting Organization

The **Contracting Organization** contracts with the performing organization to develop the product using a project discipline. The **Contracting Organization** represents two departments: Product and Technical Support. Product is divided into Sales and Advertising, Marketing and Product, and Strategic Development. A brief description of each area follows.

>   **Sales** and **Advertising:** The area that sells to ISPs, affinity groups, and advertisers, in both the domestic and international markets.

Marketing and *Product:* This area manages the portfolio of features and functionality for outbound marketing.

Strategic Development: Research and Development group viewing opportunities in emerging markets and up-selling existing accounts.

Technical Support: Technical Support performs two roles in the current environment: Training and customer support. As the *Service Organization* they provide customer support to ISP (second level) and end users (first level). In their role as the *Training Organization* they provide training to ISP field and service engineers.

Customer

A *customer* is the individual or organization who will use the project product. Note that there is a distinction for SDLC.com between the true customer and the *Contracting Organization* that acts as the customer's representative within SDLC.com.

Office of the Chief Executive (OCE)

The *Office of the Chief Executive* is the executive management team at SDLC.com. They establish business strategy and commission projects.

Owner

The *Owner* oversees the completion of work at a gate. They may be from the *Product*, *Content*, *Technical Support*, or *Development* areas depending on the project activities underway. The *Project Sponsor* assigns owners at the beginning of a project.

Each gate has an *Owner* who is accountable for tracking the gate requirements, maintaining the status of the gate and taking corrective action to ensure that the gate is met in a timely manner. The gate owner is also responsible for convening a meeting of the appropriate review board to approve passage of the gate. In the case of gates which have associated management phase reviews (see glossary), the gate owner convenes the review meeting and facilitates the decision making that is required at that gate. In the event that an exception arises at a gate which does not have any associated management phase review, the owner is responsible for escalating the issue to the appropriate management phase review board for resolution.

Performing Organization

The *Performing Organization* is generally the *Engineering* Department. The *Engineering* Department consists of Development (Sustaining, Advanced and Strategic), Validation/Quality Assurance, Operations (OCC, Release Engineering, Database Administration, Network, Unix, and Operations Engineering), Systems Engineering/Architecture and project management.

Program Manager

The *Program Manager* is the individual who oversees multiple projects that are related by a type of service delivery or by feature and functionality. The *Program Manager* is accountable for the program and is empowered by the *Office of the Chief Executive* to make decisions affecting the successful outcome of the program.

The ***Program Manager*** takes an enterprise view. He/she is responsible for determining the schedule for deployment of company resources and achieving the objectives of a specific program. The role includes the following additional responsibilities:

- Managing project managers
- Producing milestone progress reports
- Initiating issue and risk mediation
- Scheduling and conducting status meetings
- Preparing status reports
- Ensuring the on time, within budget program deliverables.

Program Management Office (PMO)

The ***Program Management Office (PMO)*** monitors, supports and reports on SDLC's programs and projects. ***Program Managers*** provide defined periodic updates to the ***PMO***. The ***PMO*** consolidates the efforts of all programs and technology specific projects and delivers these reports to the ***OCE***.

The ***PMO*** is responsible for issuing standards and guidelines for planning, tracking, and reporting, and for providing project support to individual project teams. Accountability for project delivery will remain with the individual ***Project Manager*** and ***Program Manager***.

Project Manager

The ***Project Manager*** is accountable for the project and must be empowered to make decisions affecting the successful outcome of the project responsible for managing a project. This should not be confused with the project management function that exists within many organizations.

Project Managers are responsible for determining the deployment schedule for their specific project. This role includes the following additional responsibilities:
- Reviewing progress reports
- Taking corrective action in problem solving
- Scheduling and conducting status meetings
- Preparing status reports
- Ensuring that change control procedures are being followed

Review Board

The **Review Board** is composed of representatives from both the **Performing** and **Contracting Organizations**, as well as the **Project Sponsor**, **Project Manager** and **Program Manager**. **Review Boards** assess the deliverables at each gate in the System Development Life Cycle to insure that requirements have been met. Also, the **Review Board's** specific knowledge of the project's goals and status allow it to make informed decisions to which they are held accountable.

Milestone/Gate reviews provide the mechanism for the management of the **Performing Organization** and the **Contracting Organization** to make decisions concerning the scope, cost and schedule of the project. At each review, the members of the **Review Board** are required to make decisions that are in the best interests of SDLC.com. These decisions may involve making tradeoffs to arrive at an optimal decision. It may be necessary to omit or remove scope in order to satisfy cost and schedule constraints. Additional cost may be approved to maintain scope and schedule commitments. A schedule delay may be agreed upon to enable required scope to be delivered within existing budgets. Each case is unique and must be considered on its specific merits.

Service Organization

The **Service Organization** is the unit that that provides deployment support services to the **Contracting Organization** for all SDLC products. Services include provision and support of deployment tools, software load support, problem resolution, phone support and deployment planning support. At SDLC.com the **Service Organization** is generally **Technical Support**.

Training Organization

The **Training Organization** is the organization that provides customer installation and operations training to the **Contracting Organization** for all SDLC.com products. This generally refers to **Technical Support**.

METRICS

PROGRAM/PROJECT MANAGEMENT metrics are focused on the measurement of cycle times and defects. Measurements provide the foundation to quickly identify, isolate and remediate inefficient results from activities that do not meet expected performance levels.

Cycle Time

The number of days or hours it takes to complete requirements for a SDLC BUSINESS GATE and/or milestone.

Defects

Instances of failure to pass specific tests or quality measures or to meet specification/acceptance criteria. These are recorded and assessed throughout a project and reported at the end of the project.

Change Agents

Individuals who analyze a process and recommend ways to improve it, successful or not in its adoption, will be reported to *Engineering Department* management. These individuals will receive recognition for their effort to compress cycle times and/or improve quality.

PROGRAM / PROJECT MANAGEMENT REPORTING STRUCTURE

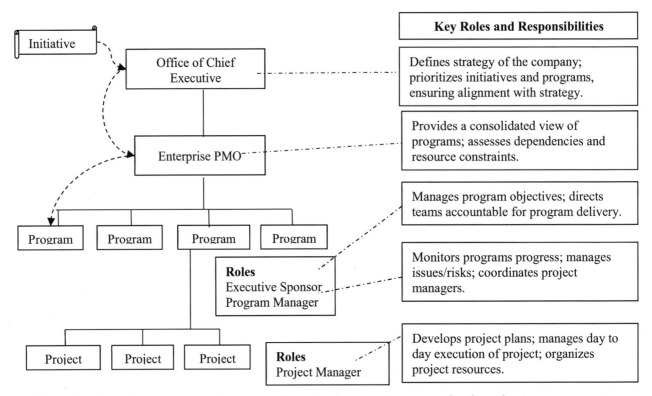

The structure above represents a reporting structure, not an organization chart.

The *Office of the Chief Executive* is the executive management team at SDLC.com. It establishes business strategy and commissions projects. *Project Sponsors* are charged with developing a concept into defined requirements and scope, and ultimately ushering the defined deliverable through project milestones. *Program Managers* oversee a portfolio of projects ensuring their successful delivery and integration into the SDLC.com environment. *Project Managers* oversee the day-to-day execution of work of specific projects, ensure that acceptance criteria are met, and manage the gate *Review Board* activities.

Project progress, issues and risks are reported to *Program Managers* who oversee a portfolio of related projects. The *Program Manager* oversees escalation, mitigation and resolution of project barriers and delays whenever a *Project Manager* requires assistance. *Program Managers* provide progress reports to the *Program Management Office* where enterprise level project plans are produced and reviewed. Impacts across program and projects are identified and reported by the *Program Management Office*.

Certain *Engineering Department* technical activities fall outside the activities specific to a project. These activities (e.g., hardware and software maintenance, tools and utilities, etc.) are reported directly to the *Program Management Office*. The *Office of the Chief Executive*

assesses these time and resource requirements via the enterprise level project plan maintained by the *PMO*.

WEEKLY REPORTING AND STATUS MEETINGS

Project Level

Each week the *Project Manager* completes a PROJECT REPORT (Appendix 4) that is provided to the *Program Manager*. At weekly status meetings *Program* and *Project Managers'* review the project report and strategize on approaches to address-identified risks and issues. Action items are developed and agreed to by the *Program* and *Project Managers.* These action items are tracked and reported on the weekly PROJECT REPORT.

Technology projects outside program delivery are reported directly to the *PMO* by the technology *Project Manager* using the same reporting mechanism as above.

Program Level

The *Program Manager* consolidates individual project reports from each reporting *Project Manager* into a PROGRAM REPORT for the *PMO*. PROGRAM REPORTS focus on the enterprise and as such present milestones, opportunities, risks and issues that are effecting efforts. In cases where *OCE* intervention is requested, course of action recommendations are included.

PMO Level

PMO meets weekly with *Program Managers* to review status reports and share information about the activities of other projects and programs. The weekly PROGRAM REPORTS data are analyzed and used to prepare the OCE STATUS REPORT. The *PMO presents the* report to *OCE* members. The *PMO* attends *OCE* meetings to address concerns and solicit assistance for *Program Manager* requests for support and/or intervention. Action items from the *OCE* meeting are communicated to the PMO within 2 days (or as appropriate).

As part of the *OCE*'s PMO REPORT technology projects outside of formal programs are reported upon. Prioritization and integration into the consolidated/enterprise project plan is determined. The *PMO* reports back to the technology **Project Manager** the results of the meeting.

PROCEDURE ACTIVITIES

G-12: Project Start

> **Business Objective:** Declare the start of the project. This gate is used to kick-off finalization of the feature set and project strategy.
>
> **Owner:**   ***Program Sponsor***
>
> **Review Board:** N/A

Project Start begins with the designation of a ***Program Sponsor*** and ***Project Manager***. The ***Program Sponsor*** is designated by ***OCE***. The ***Program Manager*** assigns the ***Project Manager***.

G-11: Project Strategy Lock-Down

> **Business Objective:** Approve a set of features and project strategy
>
> **Owner:**   ***Project Manager***
>
> **Review Board:** ***Program Sponsor, Program Manager, Project Manager, Contracting Organization(s), and Performing Organization(s)***

The ***Project Manager*** is responsible for ensuring that the following documents are completed with quality and meet the acceptance criteria defined in the **RELEASE PLANNING PROCEDURE**.

- Market Requirements Scope of Work - Owner: ***Contracting Organization***
- High Level Effort Estimate - Owner: ***Performing Organization***
- Project Strategy - Owner: ***Program Sponsor***
  - Timeline
  - R&D Budget
  - Affordability Percentage
  - Scope of Work definitions to be included in the release
  - Anchor objectives

The ***Project Manager*** establishes a preliminary project plan incorporating the project strategy and high-level effort estimates received within this gate.

Once the above documents are accepted by the receiving organization the ***Project Manager*** will call the ***Review Board*** to session and provide evidence that all requirements have been met for Gate 11. The ***Review Board*** will, at this first management review, establishes project strategy and the initial project constraints of scope, cost and schedule utilizing such factors as R & D Budget, Affordability Models and Anchor Objectives.

Upon approval by the ***Review Board***, all materials are communicated to the ***Contracting*** and ***Performing Organizations***. The communication is focused at the approved anchor objectives, project strategy, initial project constraints and scheduling. The ***Project Manager*** is responsible for communications to all participating project areas.

G-10: Requirements Scope Lock-Down

Business Objective: Approve the Scope of Work for which the organization will commit to develop requirements.

Owner: *Project Manager*

Review Board: *Program Sponsor, Program Manager, Project Manager, Contracting Organization(s), and Performing Organization(s)*

The *Project Manager* is responsible for ensuring that the following documents are completed with quality and meet acceptance criteria defined in the RELEASE PLANNING PROCEDURE.

- Initial Portfolio Scope - Owner: *Contracting Organization*
- Project Resource Plan - Owner: *Performing Organization*
- Business Plan Impact Assessment - Owner: *Contracting Organization*
- Scope of Work - Owner: *Contracting Organization*

At the start of the DEFINITION PHASE, the *Review Board* reviews the results of the concept phase and commits to the definition and planning of a project. Target delivery windows may be established, but this does not constitute a commitment to deliver the project as it is defined at this point. The additional definition and planning which takes place during the definition phase will increase knowledge about the scope, cost and schedule of the project which may result in changes to any or all of those parameters.

The *Project Manager* is responsible for scheduling, notification, meeting materials, meeting facilitation and meeting minutes for this formal *Review Board* meeting.

The *Review Board's* acceptance of the approved documents by the receiving organization moves each Scope of Work document to the Development Function of the *Performing Organization* for analysis.

The *Project Manager* ensures coordination between *Contracting* and *Performing Organizations*. *Project Managers* facilitate meetings and document meeting outcomes. This effort is focused at reducing cycle time and maintaining the highest level of common understanding between parties. Further, the *Project Manager* will refine the project plan incorporating data available.

G-9: Definition Phase Plan Approved

Business Objective: Approve the plan to execute the definition phase so that the project's business requirements (scope, timeframe and cost) are met

Owner: *Project Manager*

Review Board: *Program Sponsor, Program Manager, Project Manager, Contracting Organization(s), and Performing Organization(s)*

The *Project Manager* is responsible for ensuring that the following documents are completed with quality and meet acceptance criteria defined in the DEFINITION PHASE PROCEDURE.

- Plan for the Definition Phase - Owner: *Project Manager*

In order to complete the plan for the DEFINITION PHASE, the *Project Manager* requests and receives the items listed below from various areas of both the *Contracting* and *Performing Organizations*. Acceptance criteria for each item listed are defined in the DEFINITION PHASE PROCEDURE.

- Detailed Schedule - Contributors: *Contracting and Performing Organizations*
- Resources/Costs Assigned - Contributors: *Contracting and Performing Organizations*
- Capital Budget - Contributors: *Contracting and Performing Organizations*
- Risk Plan Developed - Contributors: *Contracting and Performing Organizations*
- Quality Plan - Contributor: *Validation Function (QA) of the Performing Organization*
- Configuration Plan - Contributor: *Operations Function of the Performing Organization*

These items contribute to the development of the project's communication plan and project plan by the *Project Manager.* At this point the *Project Manager* ensures that all known assumptions, dependencies, constraints, and risks are reflected in the project plan.
The *Project Manager* sends recommendations to minimize the impact from assumptions, dependencies, constraints, and risks to the *Program Sponsor*. The *Program Sponsor* supports the resolution and/or mitigation of project barriers by working with *OCE* and/or *unit managers*.

G-8: System Requirements Definition Approved

Business Objective: Obtain approval of the system requirements definition(s) from the Contracting Organization(s).

Owner: *Project Manager*

Review Board: *Program Manager, Project Manager, Contracting Organization(s), and Performing Organization(s)*

The *Project Manager* facilitates the dialog necessary between all parties that participated in the definition of Scope of Work documents for the *Development Function* of the *Performing Organization* to complete **Systems Requirements Specifications**. The *Review Board* reviews the approved **System Requirements Specifications**.

The *Project Manager* has responsibility for ensuring full disclosure of features, functionality and technical constraints that impact the project scope approved at Gate 10.

G-7: Lock-Down Level Estimates Complete

Business Objective: Complete the estimates and scope refinement necessary for Lock-Down.

Owner: *Project Manager*

Review Board: *Program Manager, Project Manager, Contracting Organization(s), Architecture Function of the Performing Organization(s), and Development Function of the Performing Organization(s)*

The *Project Manager* is responsible for ensuring that the following documents are completed with quality and meet acceptance criteria defined in the **DEFINITION PHASE PROCEDURE**.

- Estimation Documentation – Owner*: Architecture Function of the Performing Organization*
- Refined Resources Estimates – Owner: *Performing Organization*
- Final Portfolio Scope - Owner: *Contracting Organization*
- Work Breakdown Structure - Owner: *Development Function of Performing Organization*

The *Project Manager* ensures coordination between *Contracting* and *Performing Organizations*. This effort is focused at reducing cycle time and maintaining the highest level of common understanding between parties. Further, the *Project Manager* will refine the project plan for the release incorporating data provided through this gate.

The *Project Manager* will communicate the final portfolio scope to all interested areas in the organization.

G-6: Project Lock-Down
(Also described as: Go/No Go Decision or Cross-functional Commitment to the Delivery of a Defined Set of Features and Functionality)

Business Objective: Obtain commitment between the Performing Organization(s) and the Contracting Organization(s) for the delivery of a defined project scope of work within a defined timeframe. (This scope is a refinement of the G-10 scope/plan).

Owner: *Project Manager*

Review Board: *Program Sponsor, Program Manager, Project Manager, Contracting Organization(s), Performing Organization(s), and Service Organization*

The *Project Manager* is responsible for ensuring that the following documents are completed with quality and meet acceptance criteria defined in the REQUIREMENTS DEFINITION PROCEDURE.

- Project Plan - Owner: *Project Manager*
- Deployment Plan - Owner: *Contracting Organization*
- Service Plan - Owner: *Performing Organization*
- Business Plan Impact Assessment - Owner: *Contracting Organization*

In order for the *Project Manager* to complete the project plan, he/she will request and receive materials listed below from various areas of both the *Contracting* and *Performing Organizations*. Acceptance criteria for each item listed are defined in the REQUIREMENTS DEFINITION PROCEDURE.

- High Level Schedule Through Release General Availability - Contributors: *Contracting and Performing Organizations*
- Assigned Resources/Cost Profiles Through Release General Availability - Contributors: *Contracting and Performing Organizations*
- Approved Capital Budget - Supporters: *Program Sponsor, Contracting and Performing Organizations*
- Risk Plan - Contributors: *Contracting and Performing Organizations*
- Release Scope - Contributors: *Contracting and Performing Organizations*
- Quality Plan - Contributor: *Validation Function (QA) of the Performing Organization*
- Configuration Plan - Contributor: *Operations Function of the Performing Organization*

This gate is a significant step in the System Development Life Cycle as it is the point where both the *Contracting* and *Performing Organizations* commit to project scope, cost and schedule. Thus, prior to entering the development phase, the Review Board reviews the results of the definition phase and re-evaluates the business objectives of the project. This review may result in agreed upon changes in scope, cost and/or schedule. The resulting agreement represents a commitment between the *Performing* and *Contracting Organizations* to deliver the project as defined within the agreed upon scope, cost and schedule constraints.

The *Project Manager* is responsible for scheduling, notifying participants, creating meeting materials, facilitating meetings and distributing meeting minutes for this formal *Review Board* meeting.

The *Project Manager* ensures coordination between the *Contracting* and *Performing Organizations*. Further, the *Project Manager* communicates the project scope and schedule to all interested parties.

G-5: Detailed Plans Complete

> **Business Objective:** Approve the detailed project plan and commit the appropriate resources to execute the plan.

> **Owner:**   *Project Manager*

> **Review Board:**   *Project Sponsor, Program Manager, Project Manager, and Performing Organization*

The *Project Manager* is responsible for ensuring that the following documents are completed with quality and meet acceptance criteria defined in the DETAIL DESIGN PROCEDURE.

- Project Plan - Owner: : *Development Function of Performing Organization*
- Allocated Requirements - Owner: *Architecture Function of Performing Organization*
- System Interfaces - Owner: *Architecture Function of Performing Organization*
- Product Functional Specification - Owner: *Development Function of Performing Organization*

The Architecture Function of the *Performing Organization* includes the *Development* and *Operation* Functions since they share responsibility for delivery and support of the delivered solution. *Development* handles the creation of the interface code. *Operations* manages the receipt, processing and storage or interface data; this includes service level considerations for capacity, turnaround time, and connectivity.

In order for the *Project Manager* to complete the project plan, he/she will use the project plan from the *Development Function* of the *Performing Organization* to update the overall project plan. Acceptance criteria are defined in the DETAIL DESIGN PROCEDURE.

G-4: Begin Validation

> **Business Objective:** Ensure that the product meets the defined project scope and that the quality of the product is at an acceptable level to proceed to the Validation phase.

> **Owner:**   *Validation Function of the Performing Organization(s)*

> **Review Board:**   *Program Manager, Project Manager, Validation function of the Performing Organization(s), and Development Function of the Performing Organization(s)*

The **Project Manager** is responsible for ensuring that the following documents and activities are completed with quality and meet acceptance criteria defined in the DEVELOPMENT, TRAINING AND DOCUMENTATION, AND QUALITY FUNCTION PROCEDURES.

- Product (contains all defined scope and under configuration management) - Owner: **Development Function of Performing Organization**
- Test preparation complete - Owner: **Validation Function of Performing Organization**
- Development testing results - Owner: **Development Function of Performing Organization**
- Systems integration results - Owner: **Development Function of Performing Organization**
- Preliminary product documentation - Owner: **Development Function of Performing Organization**
- Field performance criteria - Owner: **Development Function of Performing Organization**

Gate 4 requires a formal management review by the **Performing Organization**. Before commencing validation, the quality of the product and documentation emerging from the development phase is evaluated by the **Review Board** to assess the risk associated with entering the next phase. The level of management involved at this review may be lower than at the other management phase reviews since the issues being addressed at this review are internal to the **Performing Organization**. A key consideration at this review is to determine whether the product and documentation quality is high enough to allow the testing function to make significant progress. It is also possible at this review that decisions may need to be made concerning scope, cost and schedule tradeoffs if the project performance to date has deviated from the baseline established at G-6. Such decisions should not, however, be deferred until this point in the project's lifecycle but should be actively addressed as soon as the need for a decision becomes apparent.

At any point in the life cycle, if there are decisions concerning scope, cost and schedule tradeoffs, the Gate 6 **Review Board** will formally review the situation. Should the Gate 6 **Review Board** need to assemble, the **Project Manager** is responsible for scheduling, notifying participants, creating meeting materials, facilitating meetings and distributing meeting minutes for this formal **Review Board** meeting. The **Project Manager** updates any resulting changes to the project plan. This may lead to the request and collection of revised estimates from **Performing, Contracting, and Service Organizations**.

G-3: Begin System Certification
(Product Acceptance Testing)

    Business Objective: Approve release of the product to System Certification Testing.

    Owner: **Contracting Organization(s)**

    Review Board: **Program Manager, Project Manager, Contracting Organization(s), System Certification Function of the Contracting Organization(s), and Validation Function of the Performing Organization(s)**

The *Project Manager* is responsible for ensuring that the following validation testing is completed with quality and meets acceptance criteria defined in the TRAINING AND DOCUMENTATION, AND QUALITY FUNCTION PROCEDURES.

The *Validation Function* of the *Performing Organization* completes a review and validation of the **Preliminary Documentation** provided by the *Development Function* of the *Performing Organization*. Acceptance by the *Validation Function* of the *Performing Organization* is required prior to beginning system certification. The *Project Manager* has responsibility for verifying completion and obtaining signoff from the *Validation Function* of the *Performing Organization.*

G-2: Begin FOA / Beta
(Client Acceptance Testing)

> **Business Objective:** Approve release of the product for first office application.
>
> **Owner:**   *Contracting Organization(s)*
>
> **Review Board:**   *Project Sponsor, Program Manager, Project Manager, Contracting Organization(s), System Certification Function of the Contracting Organization(s), Performing Organization(s), Validation Function of the Performing Organization(s), and Service Organization*

The *Project Manager* is responsible for ensuring that the following documents and activities are completed with quality and meet acceptance criteria defined in the QUALITY FUNCTION PROCEDURE.

- Product and Documentation - Owner: *Development Function of Performing Organization*
- Product and Documentation test results - Owner: *Validation Function of Performing Organization*
- Certification test results - Owner: *Contracting Organization*
- Implementation Deployment Plan - Owner: *Contracting Organization*
- Deployment Plan – Owner: *Contracting Organization*
- Customer Site - Owner: *Contracting Organization*
- Service Training - Owner: *Training Organization*
- Deployment Tools - Owner: *Service Organization*
- Market Analysis - Owner: *Contracting Organization*

Gate 2 requires a formal management review. The Deployment Phase represents a significant milestone to the customers in the lifecycle of a project. There is also significant risk associated with this milestone. The project product is expected to be of commercial quality at this time and any data from the validation phase that indicates otherwise must be carefully analyzed in terms of its potential impact to the selected customer site. Options at this review include approval to deploy the project product, approval to deploy with exceptions due to some subset of the scope having failed validation, and approval of a schedule delay (and consequent additional cost) to correct problems that are known to exist.

The *Review Board* reviews and approves completion of the Gate 2 requirements. Deviations in deliverables or timeframe are handled using a formal process with the results communicated by the *Project Manager* to all areas participating in the effort.

Any decisions concerning scope, cost and schedule tradeoffs, the Gate 6 *Review Board* shall formally review the situation. Should the Gate 6 *Review Board* need to assemble, the *Project Manager* is responsible for scheduling, notifying participants, creating meeting materials, facilitating meetings and distributing meeting minutes for this formal *Review Board* meeting. The *Project Manager* updates any resulting changes to the project plan. This may lead to the request and collection of revised estimates from *Performing, Contracting, and Service Organizations*.

G-1: Begin Controlled Rollout (Optional)

Business Objective: Approve the release of the product for controlled rollout. This gate is only required when a controlled rollout (CRO) is planned as an integral phase of the project.

Owner: *Contracting Organization(s)*

Review Board: *Project Sponsor, Program Manager, Project Manager, Contracting Organization(s), Performing Organization(s), and Service Organization*

The *Project Manager* is responsible for ensuring that the following documents and activities are completed with quality and meet acceptance criteria defined in the TRAINING AND DOCUMENTATION AND DEPLOYMENT AND POST IMPLEMENTATION PROCEDURES.

- Customer Site – Owner: *Contracting Organization*
- FOA test results – Owner: *Performing Organization*
- Implementation Deployment Plan – Owner: *Contracting Organization*
- Service training – Owner: *Performing Organization*
- Marketing analysis – Owner: *Contracting Organization*
- Risk mitigation plan – Owner: *Contracting Organization*
- Client acceptance – Owner: *Performing Organization*

Since a controlled rollout occurs in the production environment, the above documents must meet quality and acceptance criteria defined in the TRAINING AND DOCUMENTATION AND DEPLOYMENT AND POST IMPLEMENTATION PROCEDURES. When a controlled rollout is an integral phase of the project plan it is mandatory, otherwise, this gate is optional.

G-0: General Availability

Business Objective: Approve the release of the product for general availability.

Owner: *Contracting Organization(s)*

Review Board: *Project Sponsor, Program Manager, Project Manager, Contracting Organization(s), Performing Organization(s), and Service Organization*

The *Project Manager* is responsible for ensuring that the following documents and activities are completed with quality and meet acceptance criteria defined in THE DEPLOYMENT AND POST IMPLEMENTATION PROCEDURE.

- Product and Documentation - Owner: *Contracting Organization*
- FOA test results – Owner: *Performing Organization*
- Deployment plan complete – Owner: *Contracting Organization*
- Marketing information– Owner: *Contracting Organization*
- General Availability Implementation Deployment Plan template – Owner: *Service Organization*
- Service training – Owner: *Performing Organization*
- Order entry system – Owner: *Performing Organization*
- Customer Training – Owner: *Training Organization*
- Client acceptance – Owner: *Performing Organization*
- Market Analysis – Owner: *Contracting Organization*
- Risk mitigation plan – Owner: *Contracting Organization*

Gate 0 requires a formal review process. It is the final management phase review that occurs upon completion of initial field deployments (First Office Application and Controlled Rollout) which are intended to provide final validation of the project product in a live system environment. This review effectively marks completion of the project and acceptance by the *Contracting Organizations* from the *Performing Organization*.

The *Review Board* reviews and approves completion of the Gate 0 requirements. Deviations in deliverables or timeframe are handled by convening the Gate 6 *Review Board*. This group will make any decisions concerning scope, cost, and schedule tradeoffs.

Should the Gate 6 *Review Board* need to assemble, the *Project Manager* is responsible for scheduling, notifying participants, creating meeting materials, facilitating meetings and distributing meeting minutes for this formal *Review Board* meeting. The *Project Manager* updates any resulting changes to the project plan. This may lead to the request and collection of revised estimates from *Performing, Contracting, and Service Organizations*.

The *Project Manager* is responsible for attending the **Program/Project Management** post implementation review on the project and holds a meeting with other *Program* and *Project Managers* to review lessons learned. Trends and issues encountered over a number of projects are discussed as wells as new techniques that proved successful.

The *Validation Function* of the *Performing Organization* conducts a project post-implementation review in which representatives from all areas participating in the project review the project. Quality issues and their root cause are discussed. The **Quality Assurance** group documents the post implementation meeting and distributes to all attendees, *all Project Managers* and *Program Managers* as well as the *PMO*.

Forms

- Report Template (Appendix 4)

EXCEPTIONS

- None Known

AFFECTED/RELATED PROCEDURES

- RELEASE PLANNING
- REQUIREMENTS DEFINITION
- DETAILED DESIGN
- DEVELOPMENT
- QUALITY FUNCTION
- DEPLOYMENT AND POST IMPLEMENTATION
- TRAINING AND DOCUMENTATION
- CONFIGURATION MANAGEMENT

TOOLS/SOFTWARE/TECHNOLOGY USED

- MS Word
- MS Excel
- MS Project

APPENDIX

Appendix 1 – Glossary
Appendix 2 – Program/Project Management Detailed Process View
Appendix 3 – SDLC Business Gates
Appendix 4 – Report Template

APPENDIX 1 – GLOSSARY

Business Gate
A defined milestone in a project lifecycle when specific requirements must be met in order to make or validate business decisions relating to the project.

Lock-Down
The milestone in a project schedule achieved when agreement exists between the Performing Organizations and the Contracting Organizations for the delivery of a defined project scope of work within a defined schedule at a defined cost.

Management Phase Review
An event associated with selected business gates where specific decisions concerning the project are made by appropriate levels of management. Deviations in deliverables or timeframe are handled by convening the Gate 6 **Review Board**. This group will make any decisions concerning scope, cost, and schedule tradeoffs. These business gates are:

- G-11: Project Strategy Lock-Down
- *G-10:* Requirements Scope Lock-Down
- *G-6:* Project Lock-Down
- *G-4:* Begin Validation
- *G-2:* Begin FOA
- *G-0:* General Availability

SDLC BUSINESS GATES

The foundation of **PROGRAM/PROJECT MANAGEMENT** is the **SDLC BUSINESS GATES** (Appendix 2). This Systems Development Life Cycle (SDLC) begins at project initiation and moves through deployment to the production environment.

Phase
A collection of logically related project activities, usually culminating in the completion of a major deliverable.

The conclusion of a project phase is generally marked by a review of both key deliverables and project performance in order to determine if the project should continue into its next phase as defined or with modifications or be terminated and to detect and correct errors cost effectively.

Program
A defined set of projects containing common dependencies, and/or resources and/or objectives overseen by a Program Manager.

Project

A temporary endeavor undertaken to create a unique product or service. A project has a defined scope of work (unique product or service), a time constraint within which the project objectives must be completed (temporary) and a cost constraint. In the context of SDLC, a project may be one of:

- an individual feature
- a collection of features making up a release
- a collection of product releases making up a portfolio
- a new product development

System Development Life Cycle (SDLC)

A predictable series of phases through which a new information system progresses from conception to implementation. All of the activities involved with creating and operating an information system, from the planning phase and/or the initial concept to the point at which the system is installed in a production environment. The major phases are Release Planning, Definition, Development, Validation, and Deployment.

APPENDIX 4 - REPORT TEMPLATE

Weekly Project Status Report

Project Name:
Week Ending:
Prepared By:

Project Status and Overview

-

Milestones/Deliverable Progress This Week

-

Milestones/Deliverables Scheduled for Next Week

-

Milestones/Deliverables Scheduled for Next Week

-

New High and Medium/High Issues

-

Early Warnings, Barriers and Risks

-

Other Items

-

Standard Operating Procedure

SOP 1000-01

Title: Program/Project Management	
Effective Date:	Previous Version: None
Reason for Update: New SOP	

Owner: Chief Technology Officer	Location
Signature/ Date	

Objective   The objective of this Standard Operating Procedure (SOP) is to document the project management infrastructure, reporting relationships and project management activities. *Program/Project Managers* and the *Program Management Office (PMO)* deliver project management.

Scope   This SOP defines the SDLC project management process including structure, relationships and activities associated with the recognition, definition, design, implementation, testing, release, operation and management of a project.

Applicable To   All SDLC Product and Project Management Staff

Sections   Section 1: Roles and Responsibilities
Section 2: Metrics
Section 3: Program/Project Management Reporting Structure
Section 4: Procedure Activities
Section 5: Forms
Section 6: Exceptions
Section 7: Tools/Software/Technology Used

Attachments   Appendix A: Report Template
Appendix B: SDLC Business Gates

Related Procedures   SOP 1004: Configuration Management
SOP 1005: Release Planning
SOP 1040: Requirements Definition
SOP 1101: Training and Documentation

Definitions

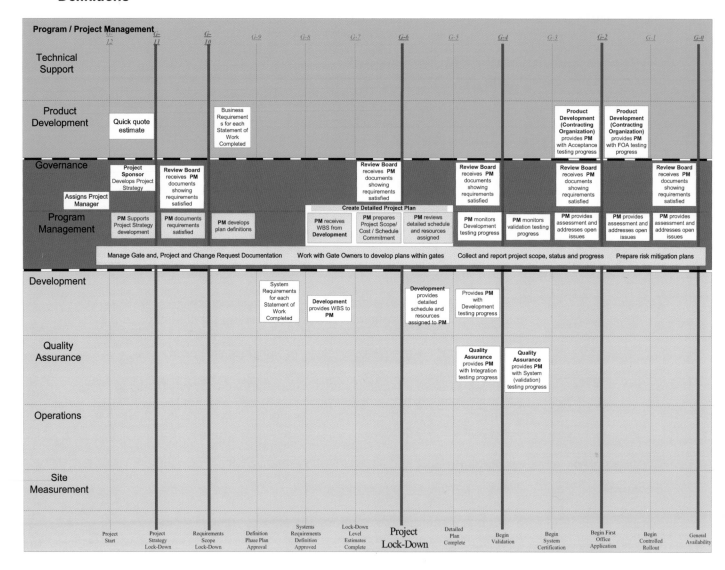

(CON) – The specified group(s) contributes to the creation of the indicated document(s)
(OWN) – The specified group(s) owns the indicated document(s)
(SUP) – The specific group(s) supports the creation of the indicated document(s)

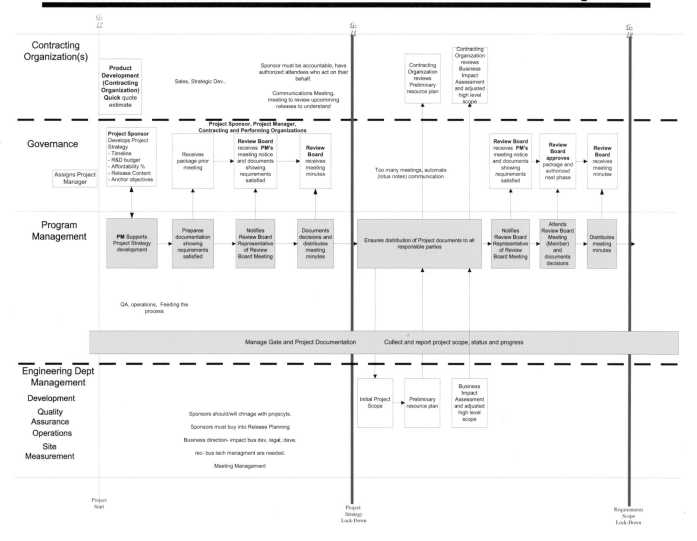

(CON) – The specified group(s) contributes to the creation of the indicated document(s)
(OWN) – The specified group(s) owns the indicated document(s)
(SUP) – The specific group(s) supports the creation of the indicated document(s)

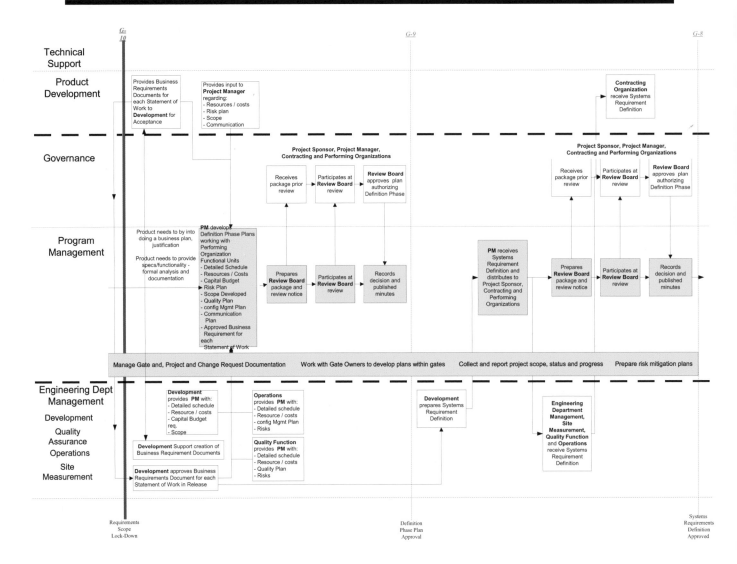

(CON) – The specified group(s) contributes to the creation of the indicated document(s)
(OWN) – The specified group(s) owns the indicated document(s)
(SUP) – The specific group(s) supports the creation of the indicated document(s)

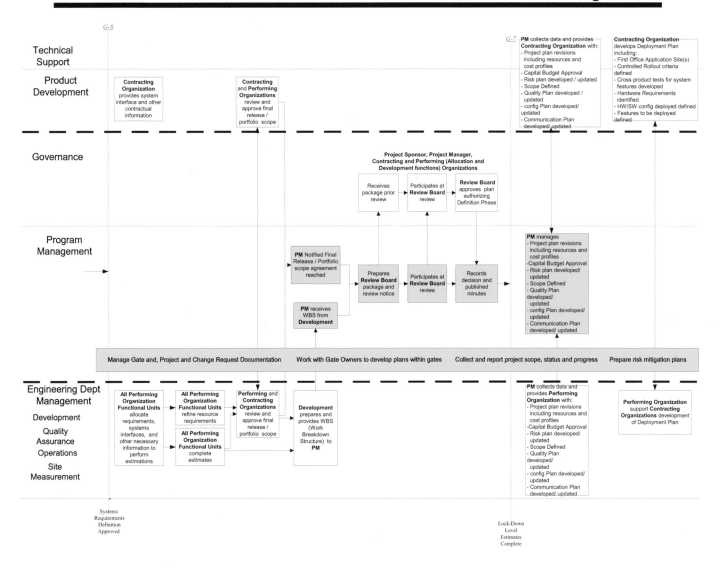

(CON) – The specified group(s) contributes to the creation of the indicated document(s)
(OWN) – The specified group(s) owns the indicated document(s)
(SUP) – The specific group(s) supports the creation of the indicated document(s)

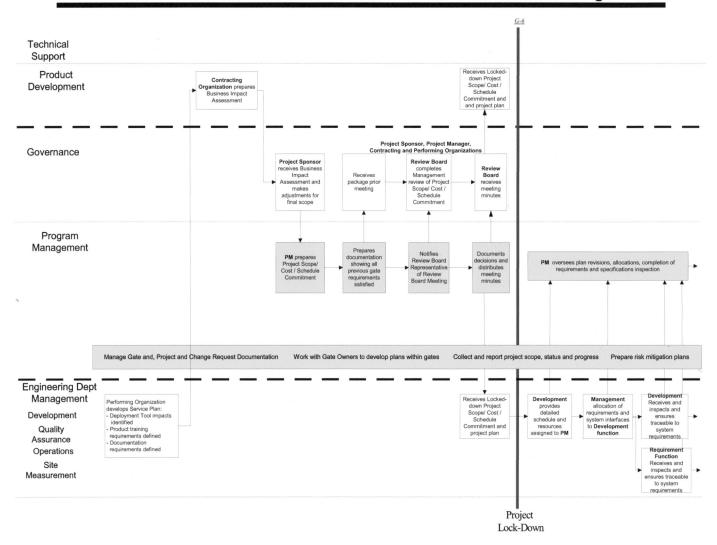

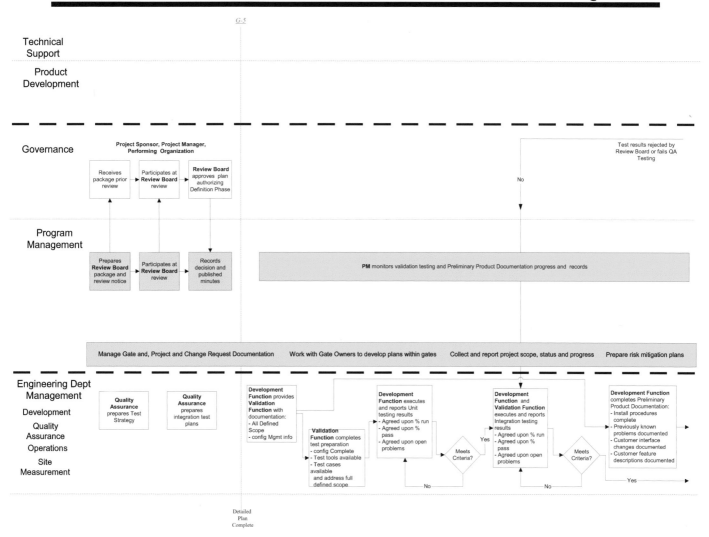

(CON) – The specified group(s) contributes to the creation of the indicated document(s)
(OWN) – The specified group(s) owns the indicated document(s)
(SUP) – The specific group(s) supports the creation of the indicated document(s)

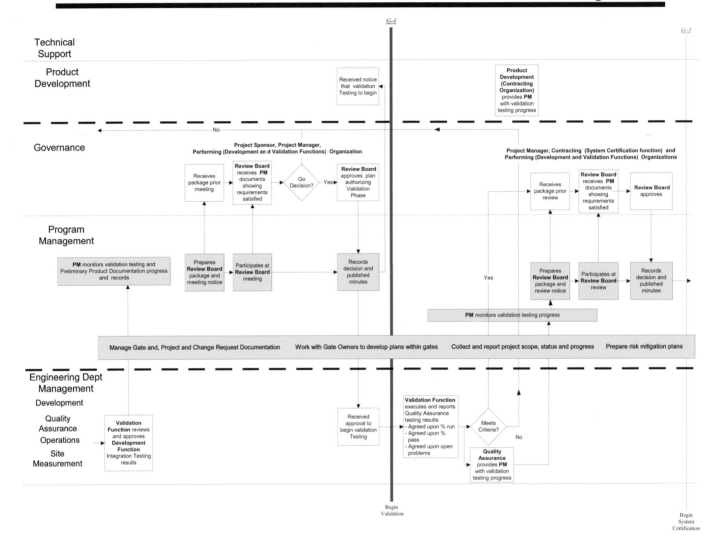

(CON) – The specified group(s) contributes to the creation of the indicated document(s)
(OWN) – The specified group(s) owns the indicated document(s)
(SUP) – The specific group(s) supports the creation of the indicated document(s)

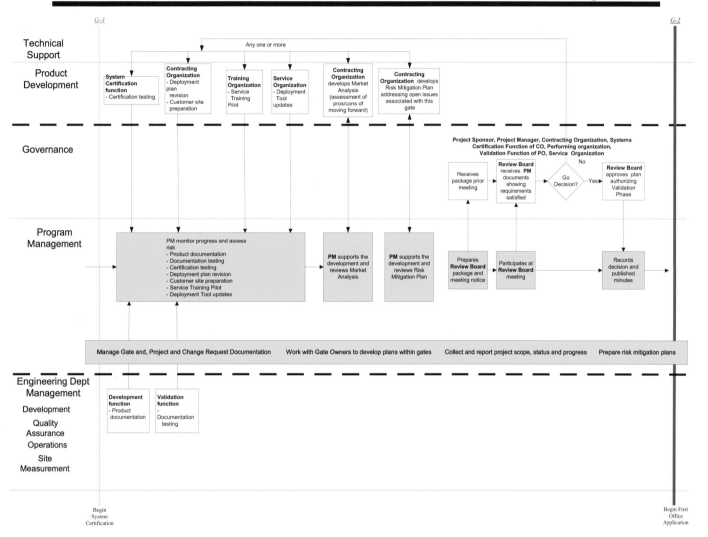

(CON) – The specified group(s) contributes to the creation of the indicated document(s)
(OWN) – The specified group(s) owns the indicated document(s)
(SUP) – The specific group(s) supports the creation of the indicated document(s)

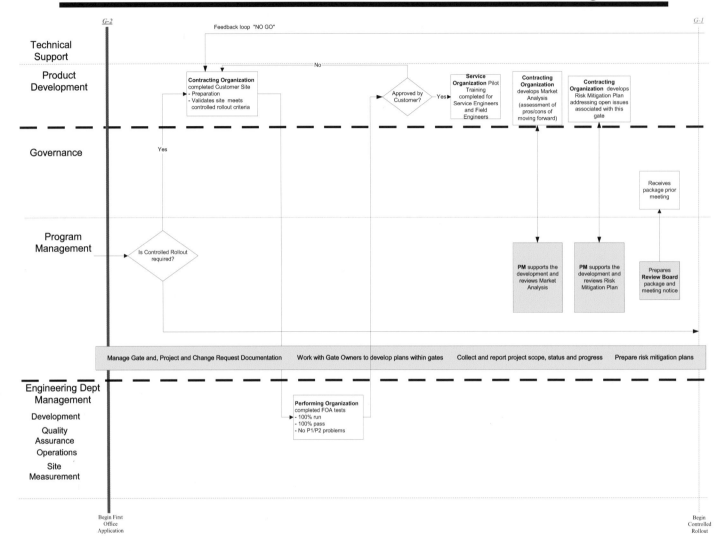

(CON) – The specified group(s) contributes to the creation of the indicated document(s)
(OWN) – The specified group(s) owns the indicated document(s)
(SUP) – The specific group(s) supports the creation of the indicated document(s)

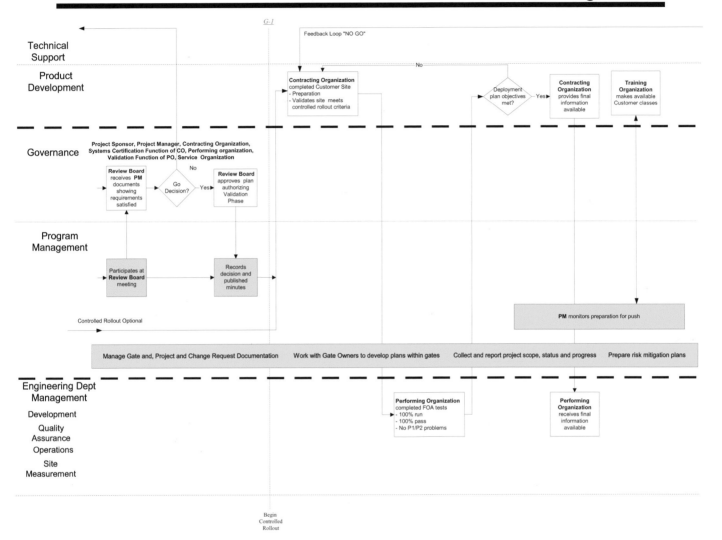

G-1

Feedback Loop "NO GO"

Technical Support

Product Development

Contracting Organization
completed Customer Site
- Preparation
- Validates site meets
controlled rollout criteria

No

Deployment plan objectives met? — Yes▶ Contracting Organization provides final information available

Training Organization makes available Customer classes

Governance

Project Sponsor, Project Manager, Contracting Organization,
Systems Certification Function of CO, Performing organization,
Validation Function of PO, Service Organization

Review Board receives **PM** documents showing requirements satisfied

No

Go Decision? — Yes▶

Review Board approves plan authorizing Validation Phase

Program Management

Participates at **Review Board** meeting

Records decision and published minutes

Controlled Rollout Optional

PM monitors preparation for push

Manage Gate and, Project and Change Request Documentation   Work with Gate Owners to develop plans within gates   Collect and report project scope, status and progress   Prepare risk mitigation plans

Engineering Dept Management

Development

Quality Assurance

Operations

Site Measurement

Performing Organization
completed FOA tests
- 100% run
- 100% pass
- No P1/P2 problems

Performing Organization receives final information available

Begin
Controlled
Rollout

(CON) – The specified group(s) contributes to the creation of the indicated document(s)
(OWN) – The specified group(s) owns the indicated document(s)
(SUP) – The specific group(s) supports the creation of the indicated document(s)

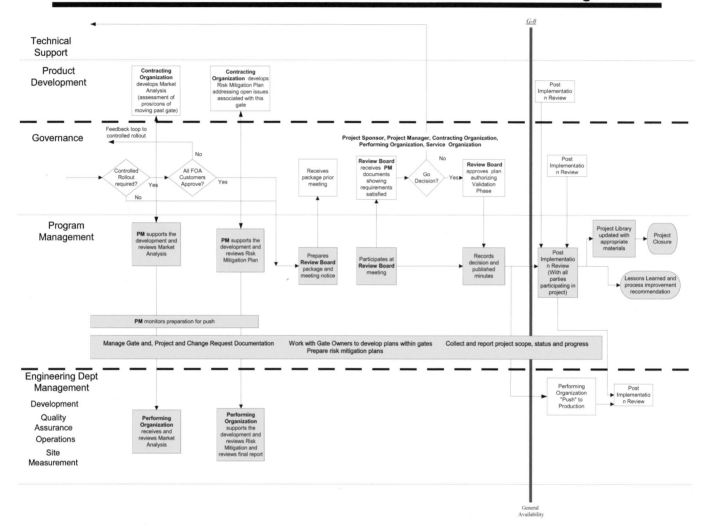

(CON) – The specified group(s) contributes to the creation of the indicated document(s)
(OWN) – The specified group(s) owns the indicated document(s)
(SUP) – The specific group(s) supports the creation of the indicated document(s)

Program/Project Management   The systematic execution of a System Development Life Cycle (SDLC) for a release or projects that have significant impact on an organization's service delivery. This procedure oversees the SDLC execution; thus, it relies heavily on defined procedure activities and acceptance criteria for inputs and outputs.

Note: Every unit within SDLC interacts with Program/Project Management. Every release of new and enhanced features and functionality requires the commitment and effort from all departments.

Project Manager   The focal point throughout a project who ensures that the responsible party has completed with quality and comply with defined acceptance criteria. The ***Project Manager*** also acts as the conduit for communicating the progress of the project and decisions made throughout the process to the ***Project Sponsor***, ***Contracting Organization***, and the ***Performing Organization***.

Program Management   Addresses oversight for a group of projects. ***Program Managers*** shoulder the responsible for the successful completion of program objectives by supporting and developing project staff. Reporting at this level provides ***Executive Management*** with the information necessary to make informed decisions and execute actions that optimize benefits to the organization.

Program Manager   The tactical manager who facilitates, monitors and communicates the progress and issues in implementing the strategic objectives of an approved program. The ***Program Manager*** works cross-functionally to develop the blueprint that integrates multiple release deliverables that enhance the program's portfolio.

PMO   The ***PMO*** is the organization that consolidates all project plans and reports the status to executive management. Impacts from individual projects can be seen from an organizational perspective and responded to rapidly. The ***PMO*** is where project and program standards, procedures, policies and reporting are established.

Business Gate   A defined milestone in a project lifecycle when specific requirements must be met in order to make or validate business decisions relating to the project.

Lock-Down   The milestone in a project schedule achieved when agreement exists between the Performing Organizations and the Contracting Organizations for the delivery of a defined project scope of work within a defined schedule at a defined cost.

(CON) – The specified group(s) contributes to the creation of the indicated document(s)
(OWN) – The specified group(s) owns the indicated document(s)
(SUP) – The specific group(s) supports the creation of the indicated document(s)

Management Phase ReviewAn event associated with selected business gates where specific decisions concerning the project are made by appropriate levels of management. Deviations in deliverables or timeframe are handled by convening the Gate 6 **Review Board**. This group will make any decisions concerning scope, cost, and schedule tradeoffs. These business gates are:

> G-11: Project Strategy Lock-Down
> G-10: Requirements Scope Lock-Down
> G-6: Project Lock-Down
> G-4: Begin Validation
> G-2: Begin FOA
> G-0: General Availability

SDLC Business Gates   The foundation is Program/Project Management in the SDLC Business Gate (Appendix B). This Systems Development Life Cycle (SDLC) begins at project initiation and moves through deployment to the production environment.

Phase   A collection of logically related project activities, usually culminating in the completion of a major deliverable. The conclusion of a project phase is generally marked by a review of both key deliverables and project performance in order to determine if the project should continue into its next phase as defined or with modifications or be terminated and to detect and correct errors cost effectively.

Program   A defined set of projects containing common dependencies, and/or resources and/or objectives overseen by a Program Manager.

Project   A temporary endeavour undertaken to create a unique product or service. A project has a defined scope of work (unique product or service), a time constraint within which the project objectives must be completed (temporary) and a cost constraint. In the context of SDLC, a project may be one of:

- an individual feature
- a collection of features making up a release
- a collection of product releases making up a portfolio
- a new product development

System Development Life Cycle (SDLC)   A predictable series of phases through which a new information system progresses from conception to implementation. All of

(CON) – The specified group(s) contributes to the creation of the indicated document(s)
(OWN) – The specified group(s) owns the indicated document(s)
(SUP) – The specific group(s) supports the creation of the indicated document(s)

the activities involved with creating and operating an information system, from the planning phase and/or the initial concept to the point at which the system is installed in a production environment. The major phases are Release Planning, Definition (Requirements and Specifications), Development, Test (Validation), and Deployment.

SECTION 1: ROLES AND RESPONSIBILITIES

Role		Responsibility
Contracting Organization	1.1	The Contracting Organization contracts with the performing organization to develop the product using a project discipline. The Contracting Organization represents two departments: Product and Technical Support. Product is divided into Sales and Advertising, Marketing and Product, and Strategic Development. A brief description of each area follows.

- Sales and Marketing: The area that sells to clients/customers in both the domestic and international markets.
- Marketing and Product: This area manages the portfolio of features and functionality for outbound marketing.
- Strategic Development: Research and Development group viewing opportunities in emerging markets and up-selling existing accounts.
- Technical Support: Technical Support performs two roles in the current environment: Training and customer support. As the Service Organization they provide customer support to end users (first level). In their role as the Training Organization they provide training to field and service engineers.

Customer	1.2	A Customer is the individual or organization who will use the project product. Note that there is a distinction for SDLC between the true customer and the Contracting Organization that acts as the customer's representative within SDLC.
Office of the Chief Executive	1.3	The Office of the Chief Executive is the executive management team at SDLC. They establish business strategy and commission projects.

(CON) – The specified group(s) contributes to the creation of the indicated document(s)
(OWN) – The specified group(s) owns the indicated document(s)
(SUP) – The specific group(s) supports the creation of the indicated document(s)

Role		Responsibility
Owner	1.4	The Owner oversees the completion of work at a gate. They may be from the Product, Content, Technical Support, or Development areas depending on the project activities underway. The Project Sponsor assigns owners at the beginning of a project.
		Each gate has an Owner who is accountable for tracking the gate requirements, maintaining the status of the gate and taking corrective action to ensure that the gate is met in a timely manner. The gate owner is also responsible for convening a meeting of the appropriate review board to approve passage of the gate. In the case of gates that have associated management phase reviews (see glossary), the gate owner convenes the review meeting and facilitates the decision making that is required at that gate. In the event that an exception arises at a gate that does not have any associated management phase review, the owner is responsible for escalating the issue to the appropriate management phase review board for resolution.
Performing Organization	1.5	The Performing Organization is generally the Engineering Department. The Engineering Department consists of Development (Sustaining, Advanced and Strategic), Validation/Quality Assurance, Operations (OCC, Release Engineering, Database Administration, Network and Operations Engineering), Systems Engineering/Architecture and project management.

(CON) – The specified group(s) contributes to the creation of the indicated document(s)
(OWN) – The specified group(s) owns the indicated document(s)
(SUP) – The specific group(s) supports the creation of the indicated document(s)

Role		Responsibility
Program Manager	1.6	The Program Manager is the individual who oversees multiple projects that are related by a type of service delivery or by feature and functionality. The Program Manager is accountable for the program and is empowered by the Office of the Chief Executive to make decisions affecting the successful outcome of the program.

The Program Manager takes an enterprise view. The Program Manager is responsible for determining the schedule for deployment of company resources and achieving the objectives of a specific program. The role includes the following additional responsibilities:

- Managing project managers
- Producing milestone progress reports
- Initiating issue and risk mediation
- Scheduling and conducting status meetings
- Preparing status reports
- Ensuring the project is on time, within budget program deliverables.

| Program Management Office (PMO) | 1.7 | The Program Management Office (PMO) monitors, supports and reports on SDLC's programs and projects. Program Managers provide defined periodic updates to the PMO. The PMO consolidates the efforts of all programs and technology specific projects and delivers these reports to the OCE. |

The PMO is responsible for issuing standards and guidelines for planning, tracking, and reporting, and for providing project support to individual project teams. Accountability for project delivery will remain with the individual Project Manager and Program Manager.

(CON) – The specified group(s) contributes to the creation of the indicated document(s)
(OWN) – The specified group(s) owns the indicated document(s)
(SUP) – The specific group(s) supports the creation of the indicated document(s)

Role		Responsibility
Project Manager	1.8	The Project Manager is accountable for the project and must be empowered to make decisions affecting the successful outcome of the project responsible for managing a project. This should not be confused with the project management function that exists within many organizations.

Project Managers are responsible for determining the deployment schedule for their specific project. This role includes the following additional responsibilities:

- Reviewing progress reports
- Taking corrective action in problem solving
- Scheduling and conducting status meetings
- Preparing status reports
- Ensuring that change control procedures are being followed

Review Board	1.9	The Review Board is composed of representatives from both the Performing and Contracting Organizations, as well as the Project Sponsor, Project Manager and Program Manager. Review Boards assess the deliverables at each gate in the System Development Life Cycle to insure that requirements have been met. Also, the Review Board's specific knowledge of the project's goals and status allow it to make informed decisions to which they are held accountable.

Milestone/Gate reviews provide the mechanism for the management of the Performing Organization and the Contracting Organization to make decisions concerning the scope, cost and schedule of the project. At each review, the members of the Review Board are required to make decisions that are in the best interests of SDLC. These decisions may involve making tradeoffs to arrive at an optimal decision. It may be necessary to omit or remove scope in order to satisfy cost and schedule constraints. Additional cost may be approved to maintain scope and schedule commitments. A schedule delay may be agreed upon to enable required scope to be delivered within existing budgets. Each case is unique and must be considered on its specific merits.

(CON) – The specified group(s) contributes to the creation of the indicated document(s)
(OWN) – The specified group(s) owns the indicated document(s)
(SUP) – The specific group(s) supports the creation of the indicated document(s)

Role		Responsibility
Service Organization	1.10	The Service Organization is the unit that that provides deployment support services to the Contracting Organization for all SDLC products. Services include provision and support of deployment tools, software load support, problem resolution, phone support and deployment planning support. At SDLC the Service Organization is generally Technical Support.
Training Organization	1.11	The Training Organization is the organization that provides customer installation and operations training to the Contracting Organization for all SDLC products. This generally refers to Technical Support.

SECTION 2: METRICS

Program/Project Management metrics are focused on the measurement of cycle times and defects. Measurements provide the foundation to quickly identify, isolate and remediate inefficient results from activities that do not meet expected performance levels.

Metric		Description
Cycle Time	2.1	The number of days or hours it takes to complete requirements for a SDLC Business Gate and/or milestone.
Defects	2.2	Instances of failure to pass specific tests or quality measures or to meet specification/acceptance criteria. These are recorded and assessed throughout a project and reported at the end of the project.
Change Agents	2.3	Individuals who analyse a process and recommend ways to improve it, successful or not in its adoption, will be reported to Engineering Department management. These individuals will receive recognition for their effort to compress cycle times and/or improve quality.

(CON) – The specified group(s) contributes to the creation of the indicated document(s)
(OWN) – The specified group(s) owns the indicated document(s)
(SUP) – The specific group(s) supports the creation of the indicated document(s)

SECTION 3: PROGRAM/PROJECT MANAGEMENT REPORTING STRUCTURE

The structure above represents a reporting structure, not an organization chart.

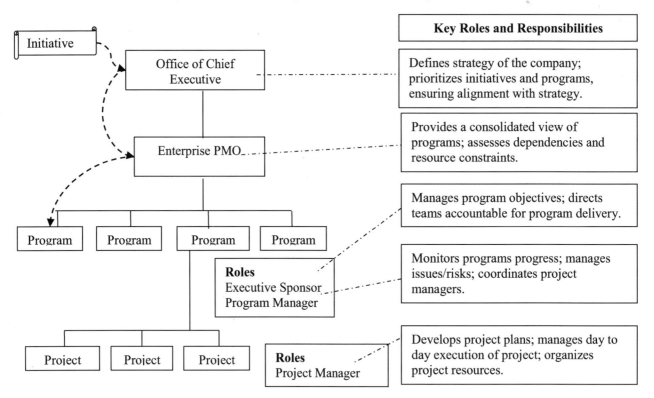

The **Office of the Chief Executive** is the executive management team at SDLC. It establishes business strategy and commissions projects. **Project Sponsors** are charged with developing a concept into defined requirements and scope, and ultimately ushering the defined deliverable through project milestones. **Program Managers** oversee a portfolio of projects ensuring their successful delivery and integration into the SDLC environment. **Project Managers** oversee the day-to-day execution of work of specific projects, ensure that acceptance criteria are met, and manage the gate **Review Board** activities.

Project progress, issues and risks are reported to **Program Managers** who oversee a portfolio of related projects. The **Program Manager** oversees escalation, mitigation and resolution of project barriers and delays whenever a **Project Manager** requires assistance. **Program Managers** provide progress reports to the **Program Management Office** where enterprise level project plans are produced and reviewed. Impacts across program and projects are identified and reported by the **Program Management Office**.

Certain **Engineering Department** technical activities fall outside the activities specific to a project. These activities (e.g., hardware and software maintenance, tools and utilities, etc.) are

(CON) – The specified group(s) contributes to the creation of the indicated document(s)
(OWN) – The specified group(s) owns the indicated document(s)
(SUP) – The specific group(s) supports the creation of the indicated document(s)

reported directly to the **Program Management Office**. The **Office of the Chief Executive** assesses these time and resource requirements via the enterprise level project plan maintained by the **PMO**.

Activity		Description
PMO Level Reporting	3.1	PMO meets weekly with Program Managers to review status reports and share information about the activities of other projects and programs. The weekly Program Reports data are analysed and used to prepare the OCE Status Report. The PMO presents the report to OCE members. The PMO attends OCE meetings to address concerns and solicit assistance for Program Manager requests for support and/or intervention. Action items from the OCE meeting are communicated to the PMO within 2 days (or as appropriate).
		As part of the OCE's PMO Report technology projects outside of formal programs are reported upon. Prioritisation and integration into the consolidated/enterprise project plan is determined. The PMO reports back to the technology Project Manager the results of the meeting.
Program Level Reporting	3.2	The Program Manager consolidates individual project reports from each reporting Project Manager into a Program Report for the PMO. Program Reports focus on the enterprise and as such present milestones, opportunities, risks and issues that are effecting efforts. In cases where OCE intervention is requested, course of action recommendations are included.
Project Level Reporting	3.3	Each week the Project Manager completes a Project report (Appendix 4) that is provided to the Program Manager. At weekly status meetings Program and Project Managers' review the project report and strategize on approaches to address-identified risks and issues. Action items are developed and agreed to by the Program and Project Managers. These action items are tracked and reported on the weekly Project Report.
		Technology projects outside program delivery are reported directly to the PMO by the technology Project Manager using the same reporting mechanism as above.

(CON) – The specified group(s) contributes to the creation of the indicated document(s)
(OWN) – The specified group(s) owns the indicated document(s)
(SUP) – The specific group(s) supports the creation of the indicated document(s)

SECTION 4: PROCEDURE ACTIVITIES

Gate/Activity	Description
G-12: Project Start	• **Business Objective:** Declare the start of the project. This gate is used to kick-off finalization of the feature set and project strategy. • **Owner:** Program Sponsor • **Review Board:** N/A
G-12a: Designate Program Sponsor and Project Manager	Project Start begins with the designation of a Program Sponsor and Project Manager. The Program Sponsor is designated by OCE. The Program Manager assigns the Project Manager.
G-11: Project Strategy Lock-Down	• **Business Objective:** Approve a set of features and project strategy • **Owner:** Project Manager • **Review Board:** Program Sponsor, Program Manager, Project Manager, Contracting Organization(s), and Performing Organization(s)
G-11a: Project Manager	The Project Manager is responsible for ensuring that the documents indicated in G-11b are completed with quality and meet the acceptance criteria defined in the Release Planning Procedure (SOP 1005))
G-11b: Organizations: • Project Sponsor • Contracting • Performing	Program Sponsor (OWN) • Project Strategy including: Timeline, R&D Budget, Affordability Percentage, Scope of Work definitions and Anchor Objectives. Contracting Organization (OWN) • Market Requirements Scope of Work Performing Organization (OWN) • High Level Effort Estimate
G-11c: Project Manager	The Project Manager establishes a preliminary project plan incorporating the project strategy and high-level effort estimates received within this gate. Once the above documents are accepted by the receiving organization the Project Manager will call the Review Board to session and provide evidence that all requirements have been met for Gate 11.

(CON) – The specified group(s) contributes to the creation of the indicated document(s)
(OWN) – The specified group(s) owns the indicated document(s)
(SUP) – The specific group(s) supports the creation of the indicated document(s)

Gate/Activity	Description
G-11d: Review Board	Establish project strategy and the initial project constraints of scope, cost and schedule utilizing such factors as R & D Budget, Affordability Models and Anchor Objectives.
G-10: Requirements Scope Lock-Down	Upon approval, all materials are communicated to the Contracting and Performing Organizations. The communication is focused at the approved anchor objectives, project strategy, initial project constraints and scheduling. The Project Manager is responsible for communications to all participating project areas. • **Business Objective:** Approve the Scope of Work for which the organization will commit to develop requirements. • **Owner:** Project Manager • **Review Board:** Program Sponsor, Program Manager, Project Manager, Contracting Organization(s), and Performing Organization(s)
G-10a: Project Manager	The Project Manager is responsible for ensuring that the following documents are completed with quality and meet acceptance criteria defined in the Release Planning Procedure (SOP 1005). Contracting Organization (OWN) • Initial Portfolio Scope • Business Plan Impact Assessment • Scope of Work Performing Organization (OWN) • Project Resource Plan
G-10b: Review Board	Responsible for scheduling, notification, meeting materials, meeting facilitation and meeting minutes for this formal *Review Board* meeting. Review the results of the concept phase and commit to the definition and planning of a project. Target delivery windows may be established, but this does not constitute a commitment to deliver the project as it is defined at this point. The additional definition and planning which takes place during the definition phase will increase knowledge about the scope, cost and schedule of the project which may result in changes to any or all of those parameters.

(CON) – The specified group(s) contributes to the creation of the indicated document(s)
(OWN) – The specified group(s) owns the indicated document(s)
(SUP) – The specific group(s) supports the creation of the indicated document(s)

Gate/Activity	Description
G-10c: Review Board	The Review Board's acceptance of the approved documents by the Receiving Organization moves each SOW document to the Development Function of the Performing Organization for analysis.
G-10d: Project Manager	The Project Manager ensures coordination between Contracting and Performing Organizations. Project Managers facilitate meetings and document meeting outcomes. This effort is focused at reducing cycle time and maintaining the highest level of common understanding between parties. Further, the Project Manager will refine the project plan incorporating data available.
G-9: Definition Phase Plan Approved	• **Business Objective:** Approve the plan to execute the definition phase so that the project's business requirements (scope, timeframe and cost) are met • **Owner:** Project Manager • **Review Board:** Program Sponsor, Program Manager, Project Manager, Contracting Organization(s), and Performing Organization(s)
G-9a: Project Manager	The Project Manager is responsible for ensuring that the following documents are completed with quality and meet acceptance criteria defined in the Requirements Definition Procedure (SOP 1040).
G-9b: Organizations: • Performing • Contracting	Plan for the Definition Phase – Owner: Project Manager In order to complete the plan for the Definition Phase, the Project Manager requests and receives the items listed below from various areas of both the Contracting and Performing Organizations. Acceptance criteria for each item listed are defined in the Requirements Definition Procedure (SOP 1040). Contracting and Performing Organizations (CON) • Detailed Schedule • Resources/Costs Assigned • Capital Budget • Risk Plan Developed Validation Function of the Performing Organization (CON) • Quality Plan Operations Function of the Performing Organization (CON) • Configuration Plan

(CON) – The specified group(s) contributes to the creation of the indicated document(s)
(OWN) – The specified group(s) owns the indicated document(s)
(SUP) – The specific group(s) supports the creation of the indicated document(s)

Gate/Activity	Description
G-9c: Project Manager	The deliverables for G-9b contribute to the development of the project's communication plan and project plan by the Project Manager. At this point the Project Manager ensures that all known assumptions, dependencies, constraints, and risks are reflected in the project plan. The Project Manager sends recommendations to minimize the impact from assumptions, dependencies, constraints, and risks to the Program Sponsor. The Program Sponsor supports the resolution and/or mitigation of project barriers by working with OCE and/or Unit Managers.
G-8: System Requirements Definition Approved	• **Business Objective:** Obtain approval of the system requirements definition(s) from the Contracting Organization(s). • **Owner:** Project Manager • **Review Board:** Program Manager, Project Manager, Contracting Organization(s), and Performing Organization(s)
G-8a: Project Manager	The Project Manager facilitates the dialog necessary between all parties that participated in the definition of SOW documents for the Development Function of the Performing Organization to complete Systems Requirements Specifications. The Project Manager has responsibility for ensuring full disclosure of features, functionality and technical constraints that impact the project scope approved at Gate 10.
G-8b: Review Board	The Review Board reviews the approved System Requirements Specifications.
G-7: Lock-Down Level Estimates Complete	• **Business Objective:** Complete the estimates and scope refinement necessary for Lock-Down. • **Owner:** Project Manager • **Review Board:** Program Manager, Project Manager, Contracting Organization(s), Architecture Function of the Performing Organization(s), and Development Function of the Performing Organization(s)
G-7a: Project Manager	The *Project Manager* is responsible for ensuring that the documents in G-7b are completed with quality and meet acceptance criteria defined in the Requirements Definition Procedure (SOP 1040).

(CON) – The specified group(s) contributes to the creation of the indicated document(s)
(OWN) – The specified group(s) owns the indicated document(s)
(SUP) – The specific group(s) supports the creation of the indicated document(s)

Gate/Activity	Description
G-7b: Organizations: • Performing • Contracting	Performing Organization (OWN) • Refined Resources Estimates Architecture Function of the Performing Organization (OWN) • Estimation Documentation Development Function of Performing Organization (OWN) • Work Breakdown Structure • Contracting Organization (OWN) • Final Portfolio Scope
G-7c: Project Manager	The Project Manager ensures coordination between Contracting and Performing Organizations. This effort is focused at reducing cycle time and maintaining the highest level of common understanding between parties. Further, the Project Manager will refine the project plan for the release incorporating data provided through this gate. The Project Manager will communicate the final portfolio scope to all interested areas in the organization
G-6: Project Lock-Down (Also described as: Go/No Go Decision or Cross-functional Commitment to the Delivery of a Defined Set of Features and Functionality)	• **Business Objective:** Obtain commitment between the Performing Organization(s) and the Contracting Organization(s) for the delivery of a defined project scope of work within a defined timeframe. (This scope is a refinement of the G-10 scope/plan). • **Owner:** Project Manager • **Review Board:** Program Sponsor, Program Manager, Project Manager, Contracting Organization(s), Performing Organization(s), and Service Organization
G-6a: Project Manager	The *Project Manager* is responsible for ensuring that the documents in G-6b are completed with quality and meet acceptance criteria defined in the Requirements Definition Procedure (SOP 1040).
G-6b: Organizations: • Project Manager • Contracting • Performing	Project Manager (OWN) • Project Plan Contracting Organization (OWN) • Deployment Plan • Business Plan Impact Assessment Performing Organization (OWN) • Service Plan

(CON) – The specified group(s) contributes to the creation of the indicated document(s)
(OWN) – The specified group(s) owns the indicated document(s)
(SUP) – The specific group(s) supports the creation of the indicated document(s)

Gate/Activity	Description
G-6c: Project Manager	In order to complete the project plan, the Project Manager will request and receive materials listed in G-6d from various areas of both the Contracting and Performing Organizations. Acceptance criteria for each item listed are defined in the Requirements Definition Procedure (SOP 1040).
G-6d: Organizations: • Contracting • Performing	Contracting and Performing Organizations (CON) • High Level Schedule Through Release General Availability • Assigned Resources/Cost Profiles Through Release General Availability • Risk Plan • Release Scope Program Sponsor, Contracting and Performing Organizations (SUP) • Approved Capital Budget QA Function of the Performing Organization (CON) • Quality Plan Operations Function of the Performing Organization (CON) • Configuration Plan.
G-6e: Project Manager	The Project Manager is responsible for scheduling, notifying participants, creating meeting materials, facilitating meetings and distributing meeting minutes for this formal Review Board meeting. *Note: This gate is a significant step in the System Development Life Cycle as it is the point where both the Contracting and Performing Organizations commit to project scope, cost and schedule.*
G-6f: Review Board	The Review Board reviews the results of the definition phase and re-evaluates the business objectives of the project. This review may result in agreed upon changes in scope, cost and/or schedule. The resulting agreement represents a commitment between the Performing and Contracting Organizations to deliver the project as defined within the agreed upon scope, cost and schedule constraints.
G-6g: Project Manager	The Project Manager ensures coordination between the Contracting and Performing Organizations. Further, the Project Manager communicates the project scope and schedule to all interested parties.

(CON) – The specified group(s) contributes to the creation of the indicated document(s)
(OWN) – The specified group(s) owns the indicated document(s)
(SUP) – The specific group(s) supports the creation of the indicated document(s)

Gate/Activity	Description
G-5: Detailed Plans Complete	• **Business Objective:** Approve the detailed project plan and commit the appropriate resources to execute the plan. • **Owner:** Project Manager • **Review Board:** Project Sponsor, Program Manager, Project Manager, and Performing Organization
G-5a: Project Manager	The Project Manager is responsible for ensuring that the documents from G-5B are completed with quality and meet acceptance criteria defined in the Detail Design Procedure (SOP 1041).
G-5b: Performing Organization	Development Function of the Performing Organization (OWN) • Project Plan • Product Functional Specification Architecture Function of the Performing Organization (OWN) • Allocated Requirements • System Interfaces The Architecture Function of the Performing Organization includes the Development and Operation Functions since they share responsibility for delivery and support of the delivered solution. Development handles the creation of the interface code. Operations manages the receipt, processing and storage or interface data; this includes service level considerations for capacity, turnaround time, and connectivity.
G-5c: Project Manager	In order for the Project Manager to complete the project plan, he/she will use the project plan from the Development Function of the Performing Organization to update the overall project plan. Acceptance criteria are defined in the Detail Design Procedure (SOP 1041).
G-4: Begin Validation	• **Business Objective:** Ensure that the product meets the defined project scope and that the quality of the product is at an acceptable level to proceed to the Validation phase. • **Owner:** Validation Function of the Performing Organization(s) • **Review Board:** Program Manager, Project Manager, Validation function of the Performing Organization(s), and Development Function of the Performing Organization(s)

(CON) – The specified group(s) contributes to the creation of the indicated document(s)
(OWN) – The specified group(s) owns the indicated document(s)
(SUP) – The specific group(s) supports the creation of the indicated document(s)

Gate/Activity	Description

G-4a: Project Manager

The Project Manager is responsible for ensuring that the documents and activities in G-4b are completed with quality and meet acceptance criteria defined in the Release Planning (SOP 1005), Training and Documentation (SOP 1101) and Quality Function procedures (SOP 1210).

G-4b: Performing Organization

Development Function of the Performing Organization (OWN)
- Product (contains all defined scope and under configuration management)
- Development testing results
- Systems integration results
- Preliminary product documentation
- Field performance criteria

Validation Function of the Performing Organization (OWN)
- Test preparation complete

Note: Gate 4 requires a formal management review by the Performing Organization.

G-4c: Review Board

Before commencing validation, the quality of the product and documentation emerging from the development phase is evaluated by the Review Board to assess the risk associated with entering the next phase. The level of management involved at this review may be lower than at the other management phase reviews since the issues being addressed at this review are internal to the Performing Organization. A key consideration at this review is to determine whether the product and documentation quality is high enough to allow the testing function to make significant progress. It is also possible at this review that decisions may need to be made concerning scope, cost and schedule tradeoffs if the project performance to date has deviated from the baseline established at G-6. Such decisions should not, however, be deferred until this point in the project's lifecycle but should be actively addressed as soon as the need for a decision becomes apparent.

At any point in the life cycle, if there are decisions concerning scope, cost and schedule tradeoffs, the Gate 6 Review Board will formally review the situation.

(CON) – The specified group(s) contributes to the creation of the indicated document(s)
(OWN) – The specified group(s) owns the indicated document(s)
(SUP) – The specific group(s) supports the creation of the indicated document(s)

Gate/Activity	Description
G-4d: Project Manager	Should the Gate 6 Review Board need to assemble, the Project Manager is responsible for scheduling, notifying participants, creating meeting materials, facilitating meetings and distributing meeting minutes for this formal Review Board meeting. The Project Manager updates any resulting changes to the project plan. This may lead to the request and collection of revised estimates from Performing, Contracting, and Service Organizations.
G-3: Begin System Certification (Product Acceptance Testing)	• **Business Objective:** Approve release of the product to System Certification Testing. • **Owner:** Contracting Organization(s) • **Review Board:** Program Manager, Project Manager, Contracting Organization(s), System Certification Function of the Contracting Organization(s), and Validation Function of the Performing Organization(s)
G-3a: Project Manager	The Project Manager is responsible for ensuring that the validation testing in G-3b is completed with quality and meets acceptance criteria defined in the Training and Documentation Procedures (SOP 1101) and Quality Function Procedures (SOP 1210).
G-3b: Validation Function of the Performing Organization	The Validation Function of the Performing Organization completes a review and validation of the Preliminary Documentation provided by the Development Function of the Performing Organization. Acceptance by the Validation Function of the Performing Organization is required prior to beginning system certification.
G-3c: Project Manager	The Project Manager has responsibility for verifying completion and obtaining signoff from the Validation Function of the Performing Organization.
G-2: Begin FOA/Beta (Client Acceptance Testing)	• **Business Objective:** Approve release of the product for first office application. • **Owner:** Contracting Organization(s) • **Review Board:** Project Sponsor, Program Manager, Project Manager, Contracting Organization(s), System Certification Function of the Contracting Organization(s), Performing Organization(s), Validation Function of the Performing Organization(s), and Service Organization
G-2a: Project Manager	The Project Manager is responsible for ensuring that the documents and activities in G-2b are completed with quality and meet acceptance criteria defined in the Quality Function Procedure (SOP 1210).

(CON) – The specified group(s) contributes to the creation of the indicated document(s)
(OWN) – The specified group(s) owns the indicated document(s)
(SUP) – The specific group(s) supports the creation of the indicated document(s)

Gate/Activity	Description
G-2b: Organizations: • Performing • Contracting • Support • Training	Development Function of the Performing Organization (OWN) • Product and Documentation Validation Function of the Performing Organization • Product and Documentation test results Contracting Organization • Certification test results • Implementation Deployment Plan • Deployment Plan • Customer Site • Market Analysis Training Organization • Service Training Service Organization • Deployment Tools
G-2c: Review Board	Gate 2 requires a formal management review. The Deployment Phase represents a significant milestone to the customers in the lifecycle of a project. There is also significant risk associated with this milestone. ***The project product is expected to be of commercial quality at this time and any data from the validation phase that indicates otherwise must be carefully analysed in terms of its potential impact to the selected customer site.*** Options at this review include approval to deploy the project product, approval to deploy with exceptions due to some subset of the scope having failed validation, and approval of a schedule delay (and consequent additional cost) to correct problems that are known to exist.
G-2d: Project Manager	Deviations in deliverables or timeframe are handled using a formal process with the results communicated by the Project Manager to all areas participating in the effort. Any decisions concerning scope, cost and schedule tradeoffs, the Gate 6 Review Board shall formally review the situation. Should the Gate 6 Review Board need to assemble, the Project Manager is responsible for scheduling, notifying participants, creating meeting materials, facilitating meetings and distributing meeting minutes for this formal Review Board meeting. The Project Manager updates any resulting changes to the project plan. This may lead to the request and collection of revised estimates from Performing, Contracting, and Service Organizations.

(CON) – The specified group(s) contributes to the creation of the indicated document(s)
(OWN) – The specified group(s) owns the indicated document(s)
(SUP) – The specific group(s) supports the creation of the indicated document(s)

Gate/Activity	Description
G-1: Begin Controlled Rollout	• **Business Objective:** Approve the release of the product for controlled rollout. This gate is only required when a controlled rollout (CRO) is planned as an integral phase of the project. • **Owner:** Contracting Organization(s) • **Review Board:** Project Sponsor, Program Manager, Project Manager, Contracting Organization(s), Performing Organization(s), and Service Organization
G-1a: Project Manager	The ***Project Manager*** is responsible for ensuring that the documents and activities in G-1b are completed with quality and meet acceptance criteria defined in the Training and Documentation (SOP 1101) and Deployment and Post Implementation procedures.
G-1b: Organizations: • Contracting • Performing	Performing Organization (OWN) • FOA test results • Service training • Client acceptance Contracting Organization (OWN) • Implementation Deployment Plan • Customer Site • Marketing Analysis • Risk Mitigation Plan
G-1c: Project Manager	Since a controlled rollout occurs in the production environment, the documents in G-1b must meet quality and acceptance criteria defined in the Training and Documentation (SOP 1101) and Deployment and Post Implementation Procedures (SOP 1220). When a controlled rollout is an integral phase of the project plan it is mandatory, otherwise, this gate is optional.
G-0	• **Business Objective:** Approve the release of the product for general availability. • **Owner:** Contracting Organization(s) • **Review Board:** Project Sponsor, Program Manager, Project Manager, Contracting Organization(s), Performing Organization(s), and Service Organization
G-0a: Project Manager	The ***Project Manager*** is responsible for ensuring that the documents and activities G-0b are completed with quality and meet acceptance criteria defined in the Deployment and Post Implementation procedures (SOP 1220).

(CON) – The specified group(s) contributes to the creation of the indicated document(s)
(OWN) – The specified group(s) owns the indicated document(s)
(SUP) – The specific group(s) supports the creation of the indicated document(s)

Gate/Activity	Description
G-0b: Organizations: • Contracting • Service • Performing • Training	Contract Organization (OWN) • Product and Documentation • Deployment plan complete • Marketing information • Market Analysis • Risk Mitigation Plan Service (OWN) • General Availability Implementation Deployment Plan Template Performing (OWN) • Service training • FOA test results • Order entry system • Client acceptance Training (OWN) • Customer Training
G-0c: Review Board	Gate 0 requires a formal review process. It is the final management phase review that occurs upon completion of initial field deployments (First Office Application and Controlled Rollout) which are intended to provide final validation of the project product in a live system environment. This review effectively marks completion of the project and acceptance by the Contracting Organizations from the Performing Organization. The *Review Board* reviews and approves completion of the Gate 0 requirements. Deviations in deliverables or timeframe are handled by convening the Gate 6 *Review Board*. This group will make any decisions concerning scope, cost, and schedule tradeoffs.

(CON) – The specified group(s) contributes to the creation of the indicated document(s)
(OWN) – The specified group(s) owns the indicated document(s)
(SUP) – The specific group(s) supports the creation of the indicated document(s)

Gate/Activity	Description
G-0d: Project Manager	Should the Gate 6 **Review Board** need to assemble, the **Project Manager** is responsible for scheduling, notifying participants, creating meeting materials, facilitating meetings and distributing meeting minutes for this formal **Review Board** meeting. The **Project Manager** updates any resulting changes to the project plan. This may lead to the request and collection of revised estimates from **Performing, Contracting, and Service Organizations**.
	The **Project Manager** is responsible for attending the **Program/Project Management** post implementation review on the project and holds a meeting with other **Program** and **Project Managers** to review lessons learned. Trends and issues encountered over a number of projects are discussed as wells as new techniques that proved successful.
G-0e: Performing Organization	The **Validation Function** of the **Performing Organization** conducts a project post-implementation review in which representatives from all areas participating in the project review the project. Quality issues and their root cause are discussed.
	The **Quality Assurance** group documents the post implementation meeting and distributes to all attendees, **all Project Managers** and **Program Managers** as well as the **PMO**.

SECTION 5: FORMS

Form		Description
Report Template	5.1	See Appendix A

SECTION 6: EXCEPTIONS

- None at this time

(CON) – The specified group(s) contributes to the creation of the indicated document(s)
(OWN) – The specified group(s) owns the indicated document(s)
(SUP) – The specific group(s) supports the creation of the indicated document(s)

SECTION 7: TOOLS/SOFTWARE/TECHNOLOGY USED

Tool		Description
MS Word	7.1	Word Processing
MS Excel	7.2	Spreadsheet

(CON) – The specified group(s) contributes to the creation of the indicated document(s)
(OWN) – The specified group(s) owns the indicated document(s)
(SUP) – The specific group(s) supports the creation of the indicated document(s)

Appendix A: Report Template

Weekly Project Status Report

Project Name:
Week Ending:
Prepared By:

Project Status and Overview

•

Milestones/Deliverable Progress This Week

•

Milestones/Deliverables Scheduled for Next Week

•

New High and Medium/High Issues

•

Early Warnings, Barriers and Risks

•

Other Items

•

(CON) – The specified group(s) contributes to the creation of the indicated document(s)
(OWN) – The specified group(s) owns the indicated document(s)
(SUP) – The specific group(s) supports the creation of the indicated document(s)

Appendix B: CyberMedia Business Gates

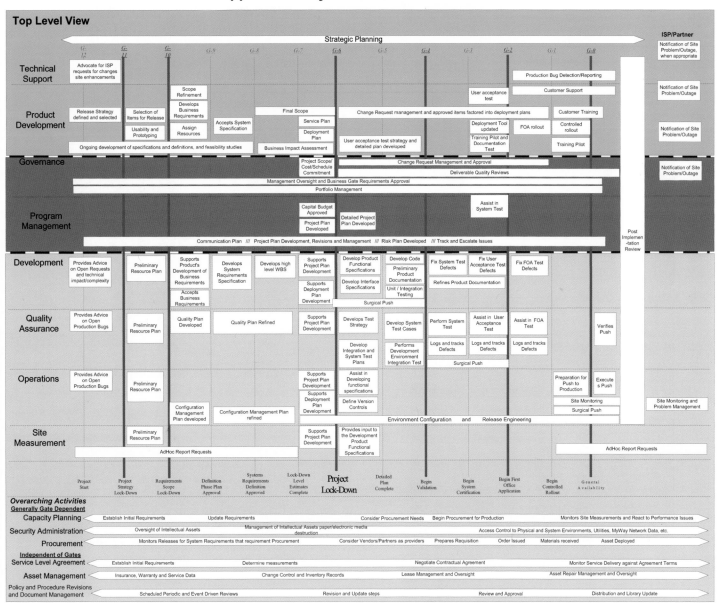

(CON) – The specified group(s) contributes to the creation of the indicated document(s)
(OWN) – The specified group(s) owns the indicated document(s)
(SUP) – The specific group(s) supports the creation of the indicated document(s)

Title: **Application Development Strategy**   Date:

Name:

Description:

Application system

Application	Development Option	Development Risk	Implementation Sequence	Risk/ Return	Remarks

Application Development Strategy

General Remarks:

Development Risk:

Assumptions and Constraints:

Title: WEB Application Maintenance Change Form   Date:

SECTION A – REQUESTOR INFORMATION

Requester: **Phone:**   **Date:**

SECTION B – CHANGE DEFINITION
DESCRIPTION: Describe the change.

REASON FOR CHANGE: Describe the reason for the change

SECTION C – PREAPPROVAL SIGNATURES

System Owner: Date:

Change Manager: Date:

SECTION D – IMPLEMENTATION CHECKLIST

Comments:

1) Change Management Opened.	Performed By:	Date:
2) Change is Developed.	Performed By:	Date:
3) Change is Tested or Staged.	Performed By:	Date:
4) Change is Released to Production.	Performed By:	Date:
5) Change Management is closed.	Performed By:	Date:

SECTION E – CLOSURE SIGNATURES

System Administrator   Date:

Technical Analyst: Date:

Security Administrator: Date:

System Owner: Date:

Change Manager: Date:

Directions:

Please fill out this form completely. It is important to provide answers that are as through as possible. Attach additional comments as needed.

Responsibilities:

1. It is the responsibility of the Requestor to initiate the change process, to coordinate the change efforts, to supply presentational elements as needed, and accept changes as a result of acceptance testing.

2. System Owners are responsible for the accuracy, relevance, usefulness, and content of web pages produced by and used with the WEB application. It is also the responsibility of the System Owner that the application meet EISS standards. The System Owner must approve maintenance changes prior to implementation and sign again to close the change.

3. It is the responsibility of the Change Manager to ensure that the appropriate forms are filled out, that the appropriate and valid approvals are obtained, and that the implementation process is followed. The Change Manager is responsible for organizing and securing change management documentation for auditing. The Change Manager must approve maintenance changes prior to implementation and sign again to close the change.

4. It is the responsibility or the system Administrator to ensure that transfer of web data from the testing/staging server to the production server is complete, timely and in accordance to any special instruction documented on the change form and supplement documents. The System Administrator is also responsible to ensure system changes that are beyond normal maintenance scope are executed only with appropriate authorization and procedures. The System Administrator must approve all maintenance changes.

5. It is the responsibility of the Technical Analyst to ensure that the application and impact definitions accurately convey the intended change. The Technical Analyst is also responsible for coordinating the development of application changes to meet the change request. The Technical Analyst must approve all maintenance changes.

6. It is the responsibility of the Security Administrator to review changes to the application that effect security control, identify security concerns, and recommend remedies. The Security Administrator must approve maintenance changes that have been identified by the Change Manager as effecting security control.

Procedure

1. The requestor fills out Section A of the "WEB Application Maintenance Change Form":

   - Requestor -The Requestor's Name.
   - Phone -The Requestor's Telephone Number.
   - Date -Date the form was initially filled out.

2. The Change Manager and Requestor jointly fill out Section B:

   - Application -The Name/ID of the application/system being changed.
   - Impact -Check blocks that apply:

     o PRESENTATION if changes are restricted to basic HTML, graphic images, electronic documents or similar non-application elements.
     o APPLICATION if changes affect HTML forms, HREF anchors populated by a database, java scripting logic, etc.

   - Description – With requestor input, briefly describe the change.
   - Reason for Change – With requestor input briefly justify the change.

3. The System Owner, then Change Manager authorize the change request in Section C of the form.

4. The Change Manager fills out section D, annotating any special requirement, and tracking the implementation of the change:

   - Change Management Opened – All required pre-approvals are obtained.
   - Change is Developed – Changed material is available for test
   - Change is tested or staged –Tested and accepted for release.
   - Change is released to production – Placed in production and archived for recovery.
   - Change Management is closed – Change completed, closure signatures obtained.

5. The Technical Analyst, if the application is impacted, directs development of application changes. The following sub-process is suggested.

   - Retrieve instance of application in development environment.
   - Apply changes to meet the requirements provided. This includes utilizing presentational elements supplied by the requestor, arbitrating remedies which best meets the design change intent, and initiating system changes if needed.
   - Place changed application in test environment for acceptance testing.

6. The System Administrator, if the application is not impacted, places presentational elements supplied by the requestor to the test environment for acceptance testing.
7. The Requestor and Tech Analyst (if required by the Tech Analyst) test the changed application and make corrections to reach an acceptance level.
8. The Tech Analyst (if required by the Tech Analyst) stores one copy of the changed application in a secured vault and provides a second copy for production release.
9. The System Administrator publishes the new application version to production, adhering to scheduling and other special instructions if required.
10. The System Administrator then notifies all approving parties of the completion of the implementation. The Change Manager changes the request by gathering closure signatures

Title: Application Request   Date:

Phone:	Name:	Requesting Organization:

Request Title:	Required By: (MM/DD/YY)	Location:	Request # (IT use only)

Requestor Name: (Print and Sign)	Date:

Department Approval: (Print and Sign)	Date:

System Owner Approval: (Print and Sign)	Date:

SUPPORT OF CORPORATE INITIATIVES:
(Check which, if any, corporate initiatives this request supports)

- ☐ Cycle Time Reduction
- ☐ Total Customer Satisfaction
- ☐ Improved Quality

REQUEST TYPE:
(Check the type of request most closely describing this request)

- ☐ Audit Issues
- ☐ Data Integrity
- ☐ Productivity/Efficiency
- ☐ Cost Improvements
- ☐ Production Problem
- ☐ Other

REQUEST CATEGORY:

APPLICATION SYSTEM:

POPI CLASSIFICATION (Required for Reports)

- ☐ General Business
- ☐ Internal Use Only
- ☐ Confidential Proprietary
- ☐ Registered Secret Proprietary

Title: Application Request   Date:

PROBLEM DESCRIPTION: (Please describe the problem and how it impacts the business. Describe both tangible (Financial, operating expenses) and non-tangible (Operating efficiencies, customer satisfaction, etc.) benefits)

EFFECTED AREAS: (List all users/organizations effected by the problem, and or by the recommended solution.)

PROPOSED SOLUTION: (Describe the recommended solution to the problem..)

COST/BENEFIT ANALYSIS: (Describe both the short term and long term cost or efficiencies gained.)

The Requester tested the solution to this request and considers the request complete

- ☐ Request/phase is complete
- ☐ With the following exceptions

REQUESTOR:	**Date:**
SYSTEM OWNER'S APPROVAL:	**Date:**
FINANCIAL MANAGER APPROVAL: (If applicable)	**Date:**

FOR INTERNAL USE ONLY

FOR ENGINEERING USER ONLY

RECEIVED BY	DATE	ASSIGNED TO	ASSIGNED ON	COMPLETED ON

CHANGE MANAGEMENT

RECEIVED BY	DATE	CHANGE MANAGEMENT NUMBER	COMPLETED ON

PLEASE ATTACH ANY SUPPORTING DOCUMENTATION, REPORT LAYOUTS, ETC., THAT WOULD HELP US EVALUATE AND ACT UPON THIS REQUEST.

Directions:

Please fill out this form completely. It is important to provide answers that are as through as possible. Attach additional comments as needed.

Item	Description/Directions
Phone	Enter the Requester's telephone number.
Name	Enter the full name of the person mailing the request. Please enter it in the format - Last name, First name.
Requesting Organization	Enter the requester's specific work group
Requesting Title	Enter a unique title for the request that can be used in all communications between IT and the requesting organizations. This title should describe the overall request clearly. It may be used to discuss the request with senior management.
Required BY	Enter the requesting organization date required for completion. ASAP will not be accepted.
Location	Enter the requester's location. (Office number and floor)
Request #	Supplied by IT once the request is submitted and all the required information is present.
Requestor Name	Enter the requester' s printed and signed name.
Department Approval	Provide the department managers approval. The manager must print and sign the form.
System Owner Approval	Provide the system owner approval. The system owner must print and sign the form
Support of Corporate Initiatives	Check one initiative that best describes the request.
Request Type	Select this from the list of' items.
Request Category	Describe the nature of the severity of the problem. Is it an annoyance? Does it cause a system to break/crash? Is data being lost?
Application System	The name of the application for which the problem was encountered.
POPI Classification	Select this from the list of' items.
Problem Description	Describe the problem/request and how it impacts the business. Describe both tangible (financial, operating expenses) and non-tangible (operating efficiencies, customer satisfaction, etc.) benefits.
Effected Areas	List all the users/organizations affected by the problem and/or benefiting from the proposed solution.

Item	Description/Directions
Proposed Solution	Describe the recommended solution (if any) to the problem n functional terms.
Cost/Benefit Analysis	Describe short term and long term costs and benefits
Requestor Approval	Once the request (if accepted as an **Engineering** project) is complete, the requester will be required to accept and sign the form. User Test Phase is a prerequisite for completing this section.
System Owner's Approval	Once the request (if accepted as an **Engineering** project) is complete, the system owner will be required to sign the form.

Title: **Asset Change**   Date:

Asset Number:

Asset Type (i.e. Server, Hard Drive, CD-ROM):

Modification or Problem:

Moved From (If applicable):

Moved To (If applicable):

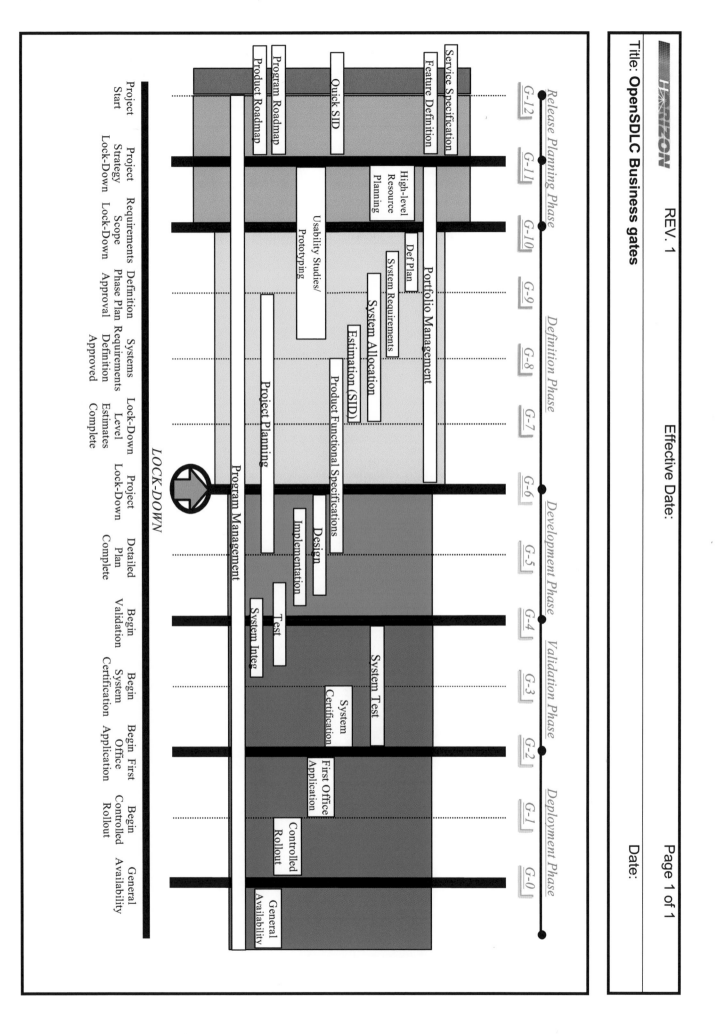

HORIZON

Title: **Business Process Performance Framework**   Date:

Mission:

Business Objectives	Critical Success Factors	Performance Measures (Targets)	Elementary Processes	Strategies

Title: Business Unit Budget   Date:

Account	Budget
	Total Budget:

Reward/Incentive:

Strengths:

Weaknesses:

Title: **Business Unit Performance Framework** | Date:

Business Unit Mission:

Business Objectives	Critical Success Factors	Performance Measures	Performance Target

Title: Business Unit Services Profile　　　　　　　　　　　Date:

Business Segments Supported:

Business Unit Management Control:

Major Business Unit Services:

Business Unit Service Characteristics:

Requestor:

Item Identification:

Reason/Project/Program for which the asset is being purchased:

Cost/Benefit Analysis, if one is required to make a "Go/No Go" decision

Title: **Change Action Summary**   Date:

Change Action	Priority (H, M, L)	Criteria for Completion/Success	Barriers	Mitigating Change Action	Enablers

Title: Change Management Request   Date:

Requester:	Ext:	C.M. #:
Date Submitted:	**Date Required:**	**Date Scheduled:**
System:	**Priority:** Low ( ) Medium ( ) High ( ) Release ( ) *Type an "X" in the parenthesis*	

Request Type: New ( ) Update ( ) Test ( ) Fix ( ) Hardware ( ) Software ( ) Stand-Alone ( ) Other ( )
Type an "X" in the parenthesis

Description:

Reason/Resolution: | **Request/Project #:**

Comments: i.e. special requirements, instructions, time needed, scheduling considerations, backup, procedures, test plan, etc.

Operator Instructions: IPL ( ) No IPL ( ) Reboot ( ) No Reboot ( ) Power ( ) Outage ( ) System Up ( )
System Down ( ) Requestor On-Site ( ) Requestor-On-Call ( ) Other ( )
Type an "X" in the parenthesis

Time scheduled:

Special Instructions: please attach detailed list if necessary

---

Disaster Recovery Instructions: please attach detailed list if necessary

---

Title: **Change Management Request** | Date:

Signatures and Dates:	
System Owner:	
Manager/team Leader:	**Technical Analyst:**
DBA:	**Security:**
Change Mgmt—Opened:	**/Closed:**
Moved/Completed:	**Scheduling Info Pulled:**

Title: Change Management Request   Date:

Directions:

Please fill out this form completely. It is important to provide answers that are as through as possible. Attach additional comments as needed.

1. Is the Requester's name and extension present?
   - This is the name and extension of the IT person requesting Change Management to implement the change.
2. Leave the CM# space blank; It is for Change Management only.
3. Is the Date Submitted present?
4. Is the Date Required present?
   - If not, is a reason / issue / concern attached?
5. Leave the Date Scheduled blank; It is for Scheduling only:
   - Is the System present?
6. Is the Priority stated? Place an "X" in the correct parentheses.
   - If HIGH, is it actually a High priority modification?
7. Is the Request Type stated? Place an "X" in the correct parentheses
8. Is the Description stated clearly, completely, concisely?
9. Is the Reason stated by an attachment identified on the line?
   - If not, is the Reason stated completely and clearly?
10. Is the Comments used for any of the following:
    - any pre-install events (db-tables, notifications, whateve1') needed? accompanying GDG Build / Change / Delete JCL ? accompanying VSAM Initial Define JCL ?
    - accompanying "Special Request" / conversion / setup JCL/DCL ? accompanying "Special$Batch" jobs to be run by the DBAs? Special schedule considerations?
    - special handling requirements?
    - special-use back-out / recovery jobs?
    - an attached task-list or special turn-over request?
    - anything unusual needed to occur as part of the install?
11. Is the Operator Instructions used for any of the following:
    - IPL needed or No IPL needed?
    - Reboot needed or No reboot needed?
    - A particular System required to be UP or DOWN?
    - Stating that the REQUESTER, who is on-call, is On-Site?
    - Someone other than the REQUESTER is On-Call?
12. That the request must go at a particular time?
13. That there are particular handling instructions, specified in detail, clearly, concisely and completely?
    - That there is an attached detailed explanation of what is needed?
14. Is the Disaster Recovery Instructions section used to specify what should occur if the install event fails?

15. *At this point print this* form. *All signatures SHOULD be hand-written.*
16. Email signatures will be accepted in cases where the signee cannot be physically reached but can send an Email as approval.
17. Is the System Owner signature present? It is needed for application changes only?
    - Did this signee review the effects of the change on the system.
    - Did the signee agree with the changes being made to the system.
18. Is the Manager / Team Leader signature present?
    - Did this signee review the package?
    - Did this signee confirm that all proper forms are included?
    - Did this signee confirm that all proper documentation is included?
    - Did this signee review to insure correct technical signoffs are present'?
    - Did this signee confirm that all items needed for the install are listed?
    - Did this signee review for proper comments for source / job mods ?
    - Did this signee review JCL for any SCAN / JCLCHECK errors?
    - Did this signee review JCL that all temp files are deleted by end-of-job?
    - Did this signee review GDG / YSAM / special setup jobs?
    - Did this signee review for compliance to naming conventions and standards?
19. Is the Technical Analyst signature present? It is required for the following:
    - Is a new CICS component needed with this install?
    - Is a CICS event required after this install, such as a "NEWCOPY"?
    - Is a new DCL logical needed with this install?
20. Is the DBA signature present? It is required for the following situations:
    - Is an SQL new or changed or deleted?
    - Is a Database element or table new or changed or deleted?
    - Is a Database impacted in any way (GEM process)?
    - Is any temp table needed for a PQL (RWC or TMP)?
21. Is the Security signature present? It is required for the following:
    - Are there any access, or privilege events happening?
    - Are there any security system owner approvals needed?
    - Are there any changes to either of the above occurring?
22. Is the Disaster Recovery Instructions section used to specify what should occur if the install event fail?

Template
Job Description

Job Title:	_____
Level:	_____
Department:	_____
Supervisor/	
Manager:	_____
Location:	_____

Purpose/Role

Key Result Area (Statement) & Outline of Supporting Activities (*These key result areas are the position's major areas of accountability and will be the basis for establishing performance measures and objectives.*)	Estimated Percent of Time Spent on Area

1.
    1.
    2.
    3.	

2.
    1.
    2.
    3.	

3.
    1.
    2.
    3.	

4.
    1.
    2.
    3.	

5.
    1.
    2.
    3.	

Resources needed to fulfill the job's responsibilities *(i.e., funds, staff, technology, access to information, etc.)*

Qualifications required to perform the essential functions of the job successfully

Qualifications	Check as Applicable	
	Minimum	Preferred/ Ideal
Education/Certifications		
Technical/Subject matter experience		
Industry experience		
Management experience		

Physical environment and requirements of the job - *Identify equipment or tools used in performing job tasks, recurring physical activity, work environment, etc.*

The purpose of this description is to provide a concise statement of the major responsibilities of this position in a standardized format. It is not intended to describe all the elements of the work that may be performed and should not serve as the sole criteria for personnel decisions and actions.

OpenSDLC.org

Title: **Continuous Improvement Framework**

Date:

Continuous Improvement Team Mission:

	Business Objectives	Critical Factors	Performance Measures	Performance Targets
Leadership				
Strategy				
Employee Participation				
Performance Measurement				
Customer Focus				

Title: Cost Benefit Analysis   Date:

Option Number:	Option Title:

Option Description:

Benefit of Option	Period 1	Period 2	Period 3	Period 4	Period 5
Total Benefits					
Cost of Option					
Total Costs					
Net Benefits/Costs					
Net Present Value					
Cumulative Benefits/Costs					
Cumulative Present Value					

Potential Implementation Costs	Software Package	Software Package with Supplementary Custom-Coded Programs	Customize Software Packages	Custom Development	Other Alternatives

Relative
Importance

	1	2	3	4	5
High					
Medium					
Low					

Current
Performance

Title: **Current Information System Description**   Date:

Name:

Type: Nature:

Description:

Owned By:

Current Information System	IS/System Under Development	Business Objectives CSFs																			

Title: Current Information System Support for Business Processes   Date:

Business Process																							
Elementary Process

Current Information System | | | | | | | | | | | | | | | | | | | | | | | |

Title: **Current Infrastructure Strengths and Weaknesses**   Date:

Infrastructure

Perceived Strengths:

Perceived Weaknesses:

Requirements	Evidence	Category	Priority (H, M, L)	Rating (Methodology: TBD)

Evidence – Why is it a requirement?
Category – Enhancement, Fix, Change, etc.
Rating – Consider customer perspective and corporate: How valuable to client? How valuable to ICST? Risk? Cost? Compliance?

HORIZON

Title: **Data Entry Usage by Location/Target Application**   Date:

Application	Location	Data Entry																		

HORIZON

Title: **Engineering Component Costs**

Date:

IT Component	One-Off Costs	Recurring Costs

Title: **Engineering Component Inventory**   Date:

Name:

Description:

Generation Level:

Performance:

Reliability:

Maturity Level:

Age: Value:

Process Use: Process Use Quality:

Title: **Engineering Infrastructure to Information System Cross Reference** Date:

IT Infrastructure / Location	Processing Architecture			Hardware			System Software			Data Management			Telecom. Software			Others:		

Title: Enterprise Competitors   Date:

Competitor Name or Competitor Group Name	Description	Remarks

HORIZON

Title: Enterprise Customers

Date:

Customer Name or Customer Group Name	Description	Remarks

Mission Statement:

Business Objectives	Critical Success Factors - CSF Description - Performance Measures - Performance Targets	Value Chain Process Areas	Strategy

Title: Enterprise Suppliers   Date:

Supplier Name or Supplier Group Name	Description	Remarks

Title: Envisioned Cultural Elements

Date:

Target Environment:

Cultural Elements	Behaviors

Equipment:		
	Facility	Facility Requirements

Date:

Equipment Infrastructure	Change Opportunity Equipment																		

Title: Facility Improvement Matrix   Date:

Change Opportunity Facility/ Facility Feature																		

Modified Feed Name:	Version:	Date:

Developer:

Type of Change:
- ☐ Major
- ☐ Moderate
- ☐ Minor
- ☐ Bug Fix
- ☐ Enhancement
- ☐ Other:

Short Description of Modification:

Database Dependencies:

Zip File Confirmed Check-In? Comments?

Code Developed Against What Database?
(Provide README HTML Document if missing.)

Provide Path to README.TXT and to ZIP file

Display Layer Dependencies:
{Where does the data show up on the site? By What Mechanism?)

Feed Schedule:

Title: **Functional Decomposition Model**　　　　Date:

HORIZON

Title: **Functional Decomposition Model**   Date:

#	Field	Instructions
1	Value chain and support process areas	The value chain and support process areas represent the top level in the potential abstraction hierarchy of enterprise activity. Value chain areas directly impact the product or service a customer consumes. The activities that comprise a value chain process area are typically operational in nature, as opposed to support.
2	Non-primitive process areas	A process area which, when decomposed, will yield lower-level process areas.
3	Primitive process areas	The lowest level process area. A primitive process area represents a grouping of enterprise activity entirely focused on one class of business object (i.e., customers, suppliers, accounts receivable, etc.) and any dependent object classes. Further decomposition of a primitive process area will yield elementary processes.

Target Environment	Current Element	Gap

Project Name:		Gate:

Project Manager:

Project Sponsor:

Deliverables: List all deliverables for this Gate including names, owners, descriptions, completion and review dates. Please include the location and name of the deliverable file with the description for that deliverable, if applicable.

Deliverable	Owner	Description	Completion Date	Review Date
R1)				
R2)				
R3)				

Title: Information System Audit Grid   Date:

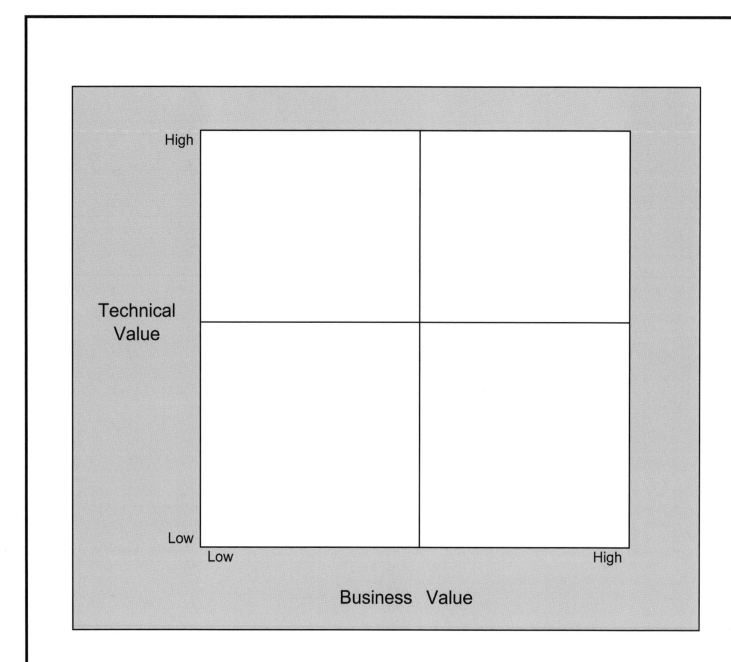

HORIZON

Title: **Information System Strategic Grid**   Date:

High

Strategic
Impact of
Current
Applications

Low

Low   High

Strategic Impact   of Applications
Development   Portfolio

Title: Information System Strengths and Weaknesses　　　　　Date:

Application:

Perceived Strengths:

Perceived Weaknesses:

Title: **IT Component Costs** | Date:

IT Component	One-Off Costs	Recurring Costs

Title: IT Component Inventory　　　　　　　　　　　　Date:

Name:

Description:

Generation Level:

Performance:

Reliability:

Maturity Level:

Age:　　　　　　　　　　　　　　　　　Value:

Process Use:　　　　　　　　　　　　　　　　　　　　Process Use Quality:

HORIZON

Title: **IT Infrastructure to Information System Cross Reference**   Date:

IT Infrastructure / Location	Processing Architecture			Hardware			System Software			Data Management			Telecom. Software			Others:		

Title: **Job Definition**

Date:

Job Title:

Tasks	Output	Tools/Facilities Required	Skills Required	Performance Measures & Targets	Relative Value Grade of Job	FTEs Required

Job Level Matrix -- Staff Professionals/Individual Contributors

Factors	Professional I (Entry)	Professional II	Professional III	Senior Professional	Consultant
Scope	Assigned tasks or phases of small projects, processes or programs. Impact of work is limited to team and phase of project.	May be assigned to small projects or to phase(s) of larger project(s).	May take on several components of a project or a complex component of a project. Work impacts quality and timeliness of project.	Work is critical to project/program success. Responsibility on complex components or complex projects may impact larger organization. May provide direction for project team. May prepare detailed work plans. Participates in defining scope of program.	May participate in the development of bus strategies and in the identification and development of bus opportunities. Develops and implements plans to meet strategic objectives within critical functional objectives or program area or recommends plan for company-wide implementation. Integrates work with various organizational units and/or multiple resources. Recommends resource needs.
Complexity	Solves routine problems using well-documented methods and techniques. Problems are limited where solutions can be readily obtained.	Exercises judgment within well-defined procedures to solve moderately complex problems with a limited number of variables.	Works beyond the routine utilizing specialized knowledge and analysis of multiple variables.	Demonstrates creativity and takes initiative in problem solving. Resolves or facilitates resolution of complex problems for assigned program.	Initiates methods and approaches to meet defined business objectives. Resolves subtle complexities that often have significant implications for program's overall success.

HORIZON

Factors	Professional I (Entry)	Professional II	Professional III	Senior Professional	Consultant
Technical/ Subject Matter Knowledge					
	Learning and beginning to apply specialized knowledge of a discipline. Applies knowledge at a basic level relying heavily on senior staff for troubleshooting.	Work requires a good understanding of the theoretical and applied basis for a discipline.	Work requires in-depth knowledge of one or basic knowledge of several disciplines. Applies principles, concepts and techniques of a discipline. May provide direction to more junior staff.	Uses knowledge of discipline and business needs to recommend appropriate action. Has an in-depth understanding of a discipline and of the interactions between various disciplines and/or functions.	Serves as lead expert in a complex subject. Recognized in and outside of the organization as a significant resource in subject area.
Supervision					
	Works under direct supervision with specific instruction.	Works under general supervision with few direct instructions.	Works under broad supervision on priorities and short-term goals.	Works under minimal supervision.	Works under general business objectives.
Experience Level					
	BA/BS degree with little or no professional experience beyond college.	Typically requires BA/BS or equivalent and 2-4 years of related experience.	Typically requires BA/BS or equivalent and 4-7 years of related and progressively more responsible experience.	Typically requires BA/BS or equivalent and 7+ years of related and progressively more responsible experience.	Typically requires BS/MS or equivalent and 7-10 years of related and progressively more responsible experience in subject area.

Job Level Matrix – Software Engineering

Factors	Engineer I	Engineer II	Senior Engineer	Principal Engineer	Architect
Scope	May be assigned to a small project or to phase(s) of larger project.	May be assigned to small projects or to phase(s) of larger project(s).	May work on several components of a project or a complex component of a project. Work is significant to project's success. May contribute to project planning.	Participates in strategic and technical planning. Helps formulate technical plans for building and integrating products. Work typically spans the scope of a complex project. May provide input to technical issues on multiple projects.	Plays an active role (leadership role) in creating a vision for the use of technology in fulfilling the company's mission. Develops high-level architectural plans.
Complexity	Solves routine problems using well-documented methods and techniques. Problems are limited where solutions can be readily obtained.	Exercises judgment within well-defined procedures to solve moderately complex problems with a limited number of variables.	Works beyond the routine utilizing specialized knowledge. Demonstrates creativity and takes initiative in solving complex problems. Solutions have implications for other areas of the project due to the intricacies involved. Seeks input from architect or project lead as issues warrant.	Solves highly complex issues often by applying new approaches.	Researches the application of advances in technology.
Technical/ Subject Matter Knowledge	Learning and beginning to apply specialized knowledge of a technology/discipline. Applies knowledge at a basic level relying heavily on senior staff for troubleshooting.	Work requires a good understanding of the theoretical and applied basis for one technology. Has developed experience in solution creation with increased business acumen.	Work requires detailed knowledge of one technology and a broader general understanding of several technologies/domains. Applies principles, concepts and techniques of technology/discipline. May provide mentoring to more junior staff.	Applies an in-depth knowledge of one or two technologies and an understanding of multiple domains (i.e., user interfaces, database, operating systems, networking, etc.) at a level sufficient to maximize their application in achieving goals. Typically provides technical guidance to others. Recognized as a technical expert in area of specialty.	Recognized as technical leader. Regarded in their field through articles, talks, etc.

HORIZON

Factors	Engineer I	Engineer II	Senior Engineer	Principal Engineer	Architect
Relationships	Receives daily guidance from Project Lead. Reports to Project Manager.	Receives daily guidance from Project Lead. Reports to Project Manager.	Receives daily guidance from Project Lead. Reports to Project Manager.	May receive general direction from Project Lead if not in that role him/herself. Reports into Project Manager. Works very closely with Project Manager to achieve goals. Works with Architect to help formulate technical plans. Mentors other engineers.	Reports to Director or VP.
Supervision	Works under direct supervision with specific instruction.	Works under general supervision with few direct instructions.	Works under broad supervision on priorities and short-term goals.	Works independently. Works toward generally defined objectives.	Works independently under broad company objectives.
Experience Level	BS degree in a related technical discipline and little or no professional experience beyond college.	Typically requires BS or equivalent and 1-4 years of related experience or MS with 0-2 years of experience.	Typically requires BS or MS equivalent and 4+ years of related and progressively more responsible experience.	Typically requires BS/MS or equivalent and 8-10 years of related and progressively more responsible experience. Should have significant project leadership experience.	Typically requires MS/PhD or equivalent and 10-15 years of progressively more responsible experience.

Job Title	Job Description	No. of Positions	Task Title	Task Description	Task ID

Product/Project Identification:	Name:	Date:

Gate/Task	Group	Activity	Lesson Learned

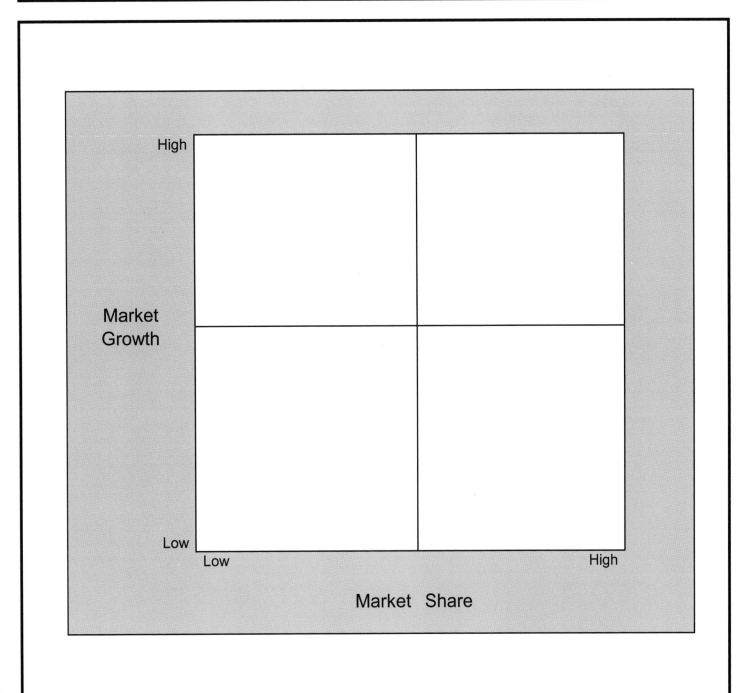

Project Name:

Objectives: List the overall objectives for the meeting such as (Review/Acceptance of Gate Deliverables)

-

Organized by:	
Location:	Scheduled Date and Time:

Attendees:

-

Agenda: List the items and issues to discuss and resolve and the time allocated to each. If applicable, identify the name and owner of an item/issue, a short description for that item and any attached documentation/files related to it.

Item) Name	Time	Owner	Description	Attachments
1)				
2)				
3)				

Meeting Guidelines:

1) Meetings SHOULD NOT exceed 45 minutes (Meetings CANNOT exceed 60 minutes)
2) Ad hoc items not involving the majority of the meeting participants should be discussed off-line
3) Ad hoc items may be discussed if the majority of meeting participants agree
4) Use of cell phones, wireless email, etc., ARE NOT ALLOWED during meetings

Meeting Organizer Responsibilities:

1) All participants have received and responded to a request to meet at the specified place and time
2) Objectives are met and all agenda items are discussed.
3) A record of the meeting activities (including an attendance log) are complete and stored in the permanent record
4) Participants assigned follow-up tasks are aware of and understand their responsibilities (including the assignment and acceptance of delivery dates/times)
5) Allocated time is not exceeded
6) Interruptions and deviations from meeting objectives are minimized

Meeting Attendee Responsibilities:

1) Acknowledge receipt of meeting request
2) Arrive at or before the specified time
3) Be prepared to discuss/address items listed in the agenda
4) Be prepared to accept one or more follow-up tasks and commit to a completion date.

Project Name:	
Organized by:	
Location	Scheduled Date and Time:
Attendees : •	

Minutes: Include items from the original meeting agenda as well as additional topics and issues discussed during the meeting.
1)
    a)
    b)
2)
3)

Action Items: List any tasks or action items defined during the meeting including: the assigned owner, a description of the item and the delivery date for the completion of the assigned item.

Action Item	Assigned Owner	Description	Delivery Date
2)			
3)			

Minutes Distribution: List the individuals to whom meeting minutes will be distributed. This includes all meeting attendees and others for whom meeting minutes are required or have been requested.

-

Minutes Attachments: List all attachments to the minutes for this meeting. This includes all attachments from the original agenda, attachments produced in the meeting and attachments resulting from completion of action items.

Attachment Name	Owner	Description
1)		
2)		
3)		

HORIZON	REV. Drafl	Effective Date:	Page 1 of 1
Title: Milestone Requirements Checklist			Date:

Project Name:		Milestone:
Project Manager:		
Project Sponsor:		

Deliverables: List all deliverables for this Milestone including names, owners, descriptions, completion and review dates. Please include the location and name of the deliverable file with the description for that deliverable, if applicable.

Deliverable	Owner	Description	Completion Date	Review Date
1.				
2.				
3.				

Title: **Mission Characterization** | Date:

Description:

Remarks:

Mission Statement:

Enterprise Objectives	Source

Industry/Market Participation	Source

Competitive Strengths	Source

Business Strategies	Source

HORIZON	REV. 1	Effective Date:	Page 1 of 1

Title: New Feed   Date:

Feed Name:		Version:	Date:
Developer:		Source ID:	

Short Description:

Feed Provider Technical Contact Information

Name:	Phone:	Email:

All feeds should be delivered as a zip file consistent with current feeds:
(Feeds should include: Installation and configuration information, batch file with scheduling information, consistent use of TNS names for database access, logging mechanism, email notification to netops mailbox, database table(s) used/modified, and simple select statement to verify successful inserts. This should be delivered in a README html document similar to xml feed.)

Provide estimate of system resources needed:
(CPU cycles and RAM requirements; storage space requirements for collected data – These items and others should be discussed at the New Feeds Interview with Director - Operations.)

Provide any other relevant information:
(Feed developed against what database? Any special instructions, including error trapping and exception handling, logging and notification?)

Display Layer Dependencies:
Where does the data show up on the site? By what mechanism? Is there a Java bean used?

Feed Schedule:

Content Updates

Content Updates:	
Content Expiration:	

Title: **Organization Map**

Date:

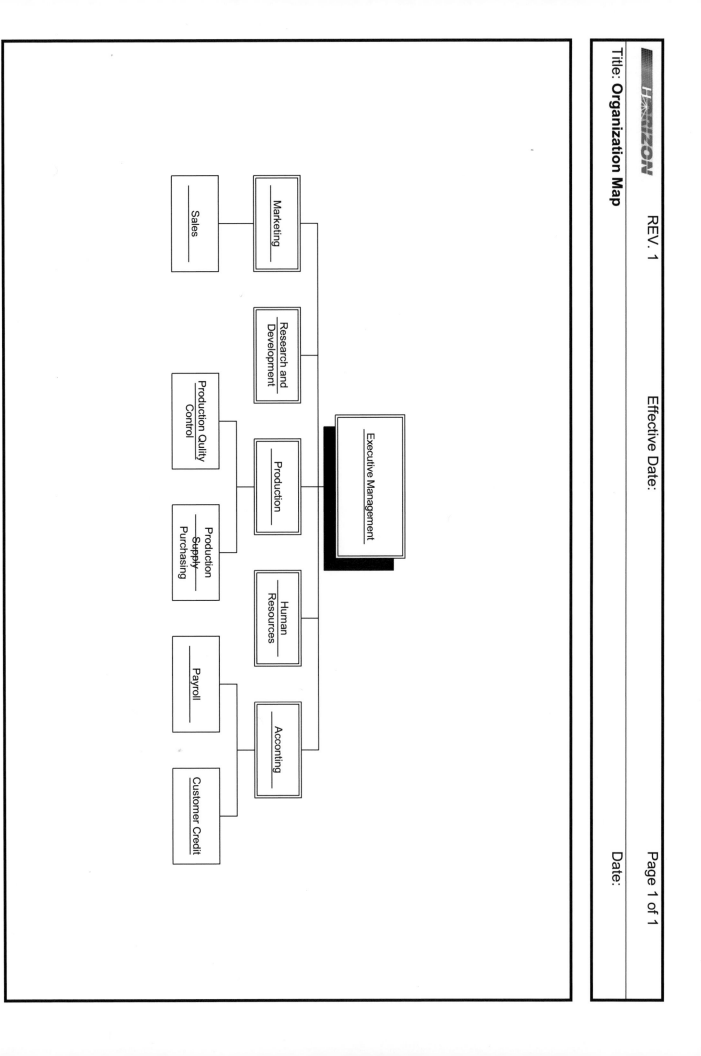

HORIZON

Title: **Package Comparison Matrix**   Date:

Requirement/Feature	Weightings				Vendor Scores			
	Level 1 (%)	Level 2 (%)	Level 3 (%)	Total	Vendor Name #1	Vendor Name #2	Vendor Name #3	Vendor Name #4

Score Totals by Vendor (computed Sum):

Title: **Potential Target Application Benefits and Risks**   Date:

Target Application:

Potential Benefits:

Quantifiable:

Unquantifiable:

Potential Risks:

Title: **Preliminary Functional Requirements List**

Date:

Target Application:

Business Process	Elementary Process	Functional Requirements	Comments	M/HD/D*

Title: **Process Design list**   Date:

Candidate Elementary Process:

Output	Output Requirements	Priority	Assigned To

HORIZON

REV. 1

Title: **Process Elimination List**

Effective Date:

Date:

Page 1 of 1

Candidate Elementary Process	Output

Title: **Product Defect Reporting** | Date:

Name:	Date/Time Defect Reported:
Organization:	Date/Time Defect Occurred:
Browser Type:	Severity Level: ❑ Emergency ❑ High ❑ Medium ❑ Low

Defect Description:

Defect Symptoms:

Steps to Reproduce Defect:

HORIZON

Title: **Project Team Membership List**   Date:

Role	Description	Assigned
Business Development		
Product Management		
Sales		
Technical Services		
Development		
Program Management		
Engineering		
Engineering (Audit)		

Total Team Members = nn

Requirements	Evidence	Primitive Process Areas				
		Elementary Processes	Elementary Processes	Elementary Processes	Elementary Processes	Elementary Processes
Total:						

Title: **Report Request**   Date:

Requestor Name:	Request Date:	Requested Completion Date:

Report Name:

Add this report to Automated Schedule:

☐ Yes (Frequency: Daily, Weekly, etc.) _____

☐ No

Distribution List for this report:

_____

_____

_____

_____

User Defined Priority:

☐ Critical

☐ High

☐ Medium

☐ Low

Description:

Business Need/Justification:

Requirements/Specifications:

- Data/Measures needed (page views, minutes, unique users, impressions, hits, etc.)

- Timeframe, Frequency (Daily, Weekly, Monthly, One Time)

- Report layout (Sort Order, Grouping, Totals)

- Delivery format (Excel file format, other)

- Delivery mechanism (e-mail, file server/LAN, hard copy)

Title: Weekly Project Status Report   Date:

Project Name:

Week Ending:

Prepared By:

Project Status and Overview:

-

Milestones/Deliverables Progress This Week

-

Milestones/Deliverables Progress For Next Week

-

New High and Medium/High Issues

-

Early Warnings, Barriers and Risks

-

Other Items

-

Title: Scope of Work   Date:

Scope of Work Information:

SOW Title	SOW Name	Requesting Organization:

Submit Date:	Requested Completion Date:

Request Type: (Check one)

☐ Enhancement: a change to an existing feature or process; a change in the way the system was originally defined in the original user requirements

☐ New Feature: a feature, service, or product to be incorporated in the system for the first time

☐ Bug/defect fix: A "bug" or "defect" occurs when the production system functionality is not performing in accordance with the Business/Users requirements.

☐ Other:

SOW Executive Summary:

Background Rationale:

Business Objectives Supported by the Request:	Justification:	Benefits:
☐ Cycle Time Reduction		
☐ Total Customer Satisfaction		
☐ Improved Quality		
☐ Other:		
Description:		

Metrics:	Financial Impact:

Title: **Scope of Work**   Date:

Deployment Requirements:

Hardware Requirements:

Software Requirements:

Hosting Requirements:

Title: **Scope of Work**   Date:

Training and Documentation Requirements:

Administrative/Help Desk Support Requirements:

Testing Requirements:

Requirement definition and feature description:

Title: **Scope of Work** | Date:

Functional Analysis:
- Use Cases

- Business Rules

- Navigation

- Page layouts

- Interfaces

- Prototype

- Usability Study Performed (required only for new features or changes to the front door)

Potential risks

Impact on current release and current customer base

- Migrating existing customers to current release

- Operational changes

- Contract/SLA changes

Title: Scope of Work   Date:

Future opportunities

Dependencies

- Impact on

- Contracts

- Partners

- Vendors

- Etc.

Interested parties/distribution list

Name:	Unit:
Title:	Required Date:

Requested Access: (Circle Requested Level)

Environment	Application	Database	Hardware
Development	RO / RW / Full	RO / RW / Full	RO / RW / Full
Quality Assurance	RO / RW / Full	RO / RW / Full	RO / RW / Full
System Certification	RO / RW / Full	RO / RW / Full	RO / RW / Full
FOA (Client Acceptance Test)	RO / RW / Full	RO / RW / Full	RO / RW / Full
Production	RO / RW / Full	RO / RW / Full	RO / RW / Full

Signature of Requestor: _____ Request Date: _____

Approving Manager has assessed the individual's knowledge and skills and certifies that the named individual meets all requirements for the security access level requested. For access beyond development, the approving manager has assessed the individual's knowledge of Company's technical environment and it meets all requirements for the security access level requested.

Approving Manager: _____ Request Date: _____

Request in compliance with approved security access profiles? Yes / No (Circle one)
        If No, is substantiating documentation attached? Yes / No (Circle one)

Sr. Security Administrator: _____ Date Received: _____

Authorizing Manager: _____ Date: _____

Secuirty Access Information:

User ID: _____ Date Executed: _____

Verified by: _____ Date: _____

Acceptance Signature (User ID delivered and accepted by):

_____ Date: _____

By signing and accepting access to Company systems environment I warrant I have completed and returned an executed non-disclosure agreement.

Area / Unit	System Environment					
Engineering	**Development**	**QA**	**System Certification**	**FOA/ Beta**	**Staging**	**Production**
Sustaining Development						
Advanced Development						
Strategic Development						
Quality Assurance						
Applications						
Databases						
Systems Engineering						
Applications						
Databases						
Hardware						
MIS Database						

Internal Departments

Content (Content Utilities)						
Technical Support						

External Entities

Exodus						
CTC Communications						

Legend: RW = Read / Write
               RO = Read Only
               Full = Unrestricted
               Exception = Full access with use restricted to request fulfillment
               W = Write (Direct write of Content to Production Database)
               W* = Write (Direct write of Content to Staging Database with automatic content update to the production
environment.)
               SU = Super User Utility to assist Web users with ID issues. Audited through review of database logs.
               None = Standard Web access only. No access to applications, databases or hardware.

Note: Sandbox environments are excluded from this procedure. Owners have control over their own environments.

Monitoring of direct content writes to production is required.

Area	Access Areas			
	Servers	**Resonate**	**Database**	**Network / H/W**
Network				
DBAs				
OCC				
Release Engineering				
Ops Engineering				
Ops Management				

Legend: X = Normal access rights for individual trained and demonstrating skills
              - = Situational exceptions requiring security to be enabled. Individuals may act in the capacity of a backup for the primary
                  individual without being a member of the specific area.

HORIZON

Title: **Service Level Agreement (SLA) Worksheet**   Date:

Service Requirement	Description	Availability	Metric
Example: Answer Phone Calls in <= 20 seconds.	All phone calls will be answered either automatically through an answering system or IVR or interactively by a call support specialist within 3 rings of the call start.	Mon – Fri 8:00am-8:00pm EST/EDT	Company phone system tracks call metrics. Monthly reports will be generated and evaluated for compliance.

Title: Service Request   Date:

Requestor Information:

Name:	Title:	Organization:

Request Date:	Requested Completion Date:

Description of Request:

Request Type: (Check one)

☐ Enhancement: a change to an existing feature or process; a change in the way the system was originally defined in the original user requirements

☐ New Feature: a feature, service, or product to be incorporated in the system for the first time

☐ Bug/defect fix: A "bug" or "defect" occurs when the production system functionality is not performing in accordance with the Business/Users requirements.

☐ Other:

Business Objectives Supported by this Request: (Check which, if any, initiatives this request supports)

☐ Cycle Time Reduction

☐ Total Customer Satisfaction

☐ Improved Quality

☐ Other:

Description:

Business Justification:

Associated Benefits: (Include a description of the metrics used to measure success)

Financial Impact and Potential Risks:

Future Opportunities:
- Functionality is being introduced during the current release, with a view to implementing further functionality during subsequent releases.

- New data being captured for which future releases could benefit

Dependencies:
- Contracts

- Partners

- Etc.

Interested Parties/Distribution list:

Title: Site Visit Worksheet   Date:

The following guidelines are based on a series of questions that may need to be raised during a site visit. Additional questions, based on specific user requirements, may have to be added to this document.

Component: Version:

Company Visited:

Visit Site – Address:

Visit Site – Telephone:

Visit Date9s):

Key Personnel Consulted:

Overall Summary:

VISIT QUESTIONS

A major purpose of a site visit is to see the software package in operation. While observing the package, determine the following:

- What is the equipment configuration?

- What part (if any) of the configuration was purchased to run the package?

- What system software is being run to support the package?
  - Operating System
  - Telecom Monitor
  - Compilers
  - Report Writers
  - Screen Painters
  - Security Software
  - Program Library Management Software
  - Special Utilities
  - Other

- Which applications had to be converted, or system software upgraded, to install the package?

- How are data entry errors handled?
  - o Numerical error code
  - o Cryptic error message/listing
  - o Clear concise message
  - o Audio signal (bell, buzzer)
  - o Other

- Does the operator often refer to an instruction manual to complete an operation, or does the system guide the operation?

- How often and for how long is the operator forced to wait for the computer to respond?

- Which reports/features does the software provide that are not being used?

Title: Site Visit Worksheet Date:

- How easily can ad hoc reports be obtained?
  - ○ Simple menu selection
  - ○ Simple parameter setting
  - ○ Complex computer-user dialog

Score: _____

Discussion Outline

1.0 Each of Installation

- What problems were encountered in adapting the package to the user's needs?

- How much time and effort was spent in the installation of the package (answer in terms of hours and elapsed time, both for the user personnel and package supplier personnel)?

- Considering Data Conversion:
  - How was the data conversion accomplished?

  - Did the installation support include file conversion programs?

  - How much time (hours and elapsed time) was required for file conversion?

- How much calendar time was required for parallel operation with the previous system and what problems were discovered with the package system?

- What problems were encountered in moving the package operation from a test to an operational environment (e.g. problems with operating instructions, etc.)?

- What problems were encountered with year end processing during testing?

Score: _____

HORIZON

Title: **Site Visit Worksheet**   Date:

1.1 Training

- What training (and how much) was required for:
  - Project team
  - Management personnel
  - Clerical personnel
  - Programming personnel
  - EDP operation personnel

- Who conducted this training and was any material supplied for on-going use?

- Where was the training conducted?

- How effective was the training provided to each group?

Score: _____

Title: Site Visit Worksheet   Date:

1.2 Documentation

- How useful was the user documentation supplied and was additional documentation required?

- How useful was the operations documentation supplied and was additional documentation required?

- How useful was the system and programming documentation supplied and was additional documentation required?

- What was the quality of the documentation content? Consider:
  - Structure
  - Whether the documentation was easy to follow
  - Index and Table of Contents
  - Precise description of operations (e.g., referring explicitly to keyboard keys to be hit rather than using "code" names.)
  - Practicality of format (e.g., binder, size, etc.)

Score: _____

1.3 Ease of Use

- How easy is the package to use (i.e., is input data easy to prepare/enter)?

- What bulk/mass maintenance features are used?

- Are the standard reports presented in useful formats? Describe briefly.

- How much clerical effort is required for input/output and control balancing?

- How many program errors were encountered? Describe nature and impact.

- Determine the frequency and quality of new program release enhancements.

- Describe any features in the package that are not used.

Score: _____

1.4 Report Writer

- Which functions is the package supplied report writer used for?

- What report writer training was provided to the user?

- What has the experience been with the report writer?

Score: _____

1.5 Throughput/Efficiency

- What throughput and/or response time problems has the user experienced?

- What are the user's present volumes for all files?

- What is the level of response times for significant inquiries?

1.6 Supplier Support

- How timely was the supplier in meeting scheduled commitments?

- How much turnover of supplier personnel was present during the project?

- Describe the promptness, quality and cost of service to alleviate errors?

- How does the user rate the supplier's attitude, co-operation and willingness to help?

Overall Satisfaction

- What has been the worst experience encountered by the user implementing and operating the package system?

- What is the users overall evaluation of the strengths and weaknesses of this package? If the user had to do it over again, what would be done differently?

Score: _____

Title: **Strategy Characterization: Market Segment Approach** Date:

Market Segment	Product/Service	Approach Justification	CSFs	Timing	Source

Title: **Strategy Characterization: Market Segment Selection**

Date:

Market Segment	Rationale			Key Competitive Capabilities	Source
	Current Mkt. Size	Forecast Mkt. Size	Growth Rate	Profitability	

HORIZON

REV. 1.1

Title: **Strategy Implementation Plan**

Effective Date:

Page 1 of 1

Date:

Action	Timing	Performance Measures/Targets	Resources	Accountability

Title: **Target Application Estimated Costs** | Date:

Target Application:

Description:

Development Estimates

Implementation Effort:

Implementation Duration:

Annual Maintenance:

Remarks:

HORIZON

Title: **Target Application Support for Business Processes**   Date:

Business Process									
Elementary Process									
Target Application Systems									

Title: **Target Application Support for CSFs**   Date:

Critical Success Factors							Weighted Total
Target Application CFS Weight							100%

Title: **Target Application to IT Component Cross Reference**   Date:

Technology Components Target Application	Implement. Option	Processing Distribution	Data Management	Telecom. Options	Graphics	Security	Others

HORIZON

Title: **Target Environment Definition Summary**   Date:

Target Element	Implication for Other Elements	TED Change Required?	TED Change Made?	Date

Title: Technical Design   Date:

Requirement Name:			Date:
Developer:	Accepted by QA ☐ Yes ☐ No	Checked into Project Folder ☐ Yes ☐ No	Checked into VOB ☐ Yes ☐ No

Short Description:

Technical Description:

Estimate of Analysis of System Impact:
(Please include CPU cycles, RAM requirements, storage space requirements, database issues, etc.)

- Tables

- Field Names

- Site Performance Impact

- Other

Title: **Technical Design**   Date:

Provide any other relevant information
(Any special instructions, including error trapping and exception handling, logging and notification?)

Display Layer Dependencies
(Where does the data show up on the site? By what mechanism?)

Recommended Test Cases (QA)
(Assumed to have been unit tested by Developer)

Title: Training Evaluation Date:

Course Title:	Instructor:	Date:

INSTRUCTIONS: Please rate each of the following items on a scale or "1" to "10" from "NEEDS WORK" to "OUTSTANDING". Circle the number which most closely represents your opinion. If the item in not applicable, circle "n/a".

COURSE EVALUATION: I would rate the following course items:

	NEEDS WORK								OUTSTANDING		
1. The participant manual	1	2	3	4	5	6	7	8	9	10	n/a
2. The quality of video tapes	1	2	3	4	5	6	7	8	9	10	n/a
3. The preparation of overheads	1	2	3	4	5	6	7	8	9	10	n/a
4. The participant activities	1	2	3	4	5	6	7	8	9	10	n/a
5. The participant discussion	1	2	3	4	5	6	7	8	9	10	n/a
6. The classroom environment	1	2	3	4	5	6	7	8	9	10	n/a
7. The seating arrangement	1	2	3	4	5	6	7	8	9	10	n/a

INSTRUCTOR EVALUATION: I would rate the instructor as follows:

	NEEDS WORK								OUTSTANDING		
8. Making material clear	1	2	3	4	5	6	7	8	9	10	n/a
9. Confidence as an instructor	1	2	3	4	5	6	7	8	9	10	n/a
10. Answering questions	1	2	3	4	5	6	7	8	9	10	n/a
11. Use of audio visuals	1	2	3	4	5	6	7	8	9	10	n/a
12. Enthusiasm for subject	1	2	3	4	5	6	7	8	9	10	n/a
13. Use of classroom time	1	2	3	4	5	6	7	8	9	10	n/a

PERSONAL VALUE: I would rate this experience as follows:

	LOW								HIGH		
14. Value to me	1	2	3	4	5	6	7	8	9	10	n/a
15. Value for my job	1	2	3	4	5	6	7	8	9	10	n/a

16. Was the material in this course:

☐ Too Theoretical
☐ At My Level
☐ Too Simple
☐ Other:

.

Comments:

COURSE DATA: *(Please answer the following questions about the content of the course. Any suggestions you offer would be greatly appreciated in helping us make sure that this course meets your needs.)*

17. What items or areas of information would you like to see added to this course that might assist you in the responsibilities of your current job?

18. What items or areas of information would you like to see removed from this course, and why?

19. What needs do you feel for other training?

20. Any other comments?

Title: **Vendor Selection Summary**   Date:

Vendor/Alternative	Site Selection Criteria/Weight					Total Score	Rank

Organizational Dimension	Vision Element	Critical Success Factor	Performance Measure	Performance Target

Title: **Weighted Requirements Ranking** | | Date:

Requirements	Customer (Weight)				Total Weighted Score	Overall Weighted Rank	Priority
	( )	( )	( )	( )			

Printed in Great Britain
by Amazon

36519438R00110